The Fundamentals of
SYNTHESIZER PROGRAMMING
SECOND EDITION

Dr. Joseph Akins

Edited by Alan Gary Campbell

The Fundamentals of Synthesizer Programming provides an introduction on how to program a synthesizer for creating music in the studio and on stage. Used as a textbook for the introductory electronic music course at the Department of Recording Industry at Middle Tennessee State University, it covers the components and controls, of both hardware and software synthesizers, that are used to create a patch on a typical synth. Concepts are explained thoroughly with block diagramming, and practical examples are given with Reason Studios Subtractor and a Moog Voyager.

Dr. Joseph Akins started as a keyboard player. Today, he is an active composer, pianist and professor. At Middle Tennessee State University, he teaches courses in the Department of Recording Industry, particularly subjects in electronic music. He has an extensive discography of recorded music that has earned various awards and extensive airplay. In addition, he has created factory patches for Dave Smith Instruments and created tutorial videos for Moog Music.

www.themidiprofessor.com - instructional products for music technology
www.josephakins.com- piano music from Joseph Akins
www.mtsu.edu/~record - the Department of Recording Industry at MTSU

Acknowledgments

Many people have contributed to the manifestation of this book. First, I must give thanks to all my teachers at the University of Tennessee, Radford University and Tennessee State. Second, to all the musicians, engineers and authors who have helped me, such as Alan Gary Campbell, the editor of this book. Third, thanks to my colleagues at the Department of Recording Industry at Middle Tennessee State University, such as Bob Wood, Jim Piekarski, Misty Simpson and Dale Brown. They helped design the electronic music courses in which this book evolved from. And last, thanks to my mom for the Roland SH-2000 on my 16th birthday!

Published by The MIDI Professor
Middle Tennessee State University
© 2010 Dr. Joseph Akins First Edition
© 2021 Dr. Joseph Akins Second Edition
jakins@mtsu.edu

ISBN: 978-0-9834960-4-5

TABLE OF CONTENTS

1		**The Fundamentals of Synthesis**
1		Introduction
1		My First Synthesizer
2		Sounds vs. Patches: The Modular Synthesizer
4		This Book Covers Subtractive Synthesis
4		Two Signal Types
4		Module Types
6		Input and Outputs
7		The Basic Model for Subtractive Synthesis
7		The Properties of Sound
9		Summary
10		Questions for Chapter 1
11		**Sources**
11		Introduction
11		The Oscillator
12		Oscillator Controls for Pitch
13		Oscillator Controls for Harmonic Content
17		Noise Generator (NG)
18		Combining Waveforms
21		Advanced Oscillator Functions
24		Summary
25		Questions for Chapter 2
27		**Modifiers**
27		Introduction
27		The Filter
28		Filter Types
31		Filter Cutoff & Center Frequencies
32		Filter Slope
33		Filter Resonance
34		The Amplifier
35		Summary
36		Questions for Chapter 3

37	**Controllers**
37	Introduction
38	The Envelope Generator
41	The Filter EG
43	Other Uses for the EG
44	Single-Trigger vs. Multi-Trigger
45	The Low Frequency Oscillator
48	Sample-and-Hold
49	The Keyboard
52	Summary
53	Questions for Chapter 4
55	**An Overview of Electronic Music History**
55	The Beginnings
56	The Experimental Period
58	The Modern Era
62	References and Further Reading for History
63	Questions for Electronic Music History
64	Notes

A Note about the Synthesizers

Two synthesizers are used for many examples in this book: Reason Studios Subtractor and the Moog Voyager. The concepts for both can be transferred to most any common synthesizer. However, Subtractor can be obtained inexpensively from *www.reasonstudios.com*. It is included with all versions of Reason, including the least expensive Reason Intro. You can purchase it there or try it free for 30 days. Reason can be used standalone or as a plug-in within your DAW.

ONE

The Fundamentals of Synthesis

This chapter is divided into eleven sections:
1. Introduction
2. My First Synthesizer
3. Sounds vs. Patches: The Modular Synthesizer
4. This Book Covers Subtractive Synthesis
5. Two Signal Types
6. Module Types
7. Inputs and Outputs
8. The Basic Model for Subtractive Synthesis
9. The Properties of Sound
10. Summary
11. Questions for Chapter One

Introduction

The fundamentals of synthesizer programming, or "synthesis," encompass how all the components of a synthesizer work together to create sounds. Once you learn the fundamentals in this book, you will be able to create your own sounds and modify sounds created by others, and will have a solid foundation through which to increase your skills at synthesis for years to come.

All the various functions found on the panel of a synthesizer, how they are interconnected, and how they interact will become understandable to you. This will allow you to go much deeper than merely using preexisting sounds (factory patches). You will become able to tweak a factory patch or create a sound entirely from scratch.

If you are a composer, songwriter, producer, merchandiser, audio engineer, keyboard player, or other music professional, you will benefit from learning these fundamentals. The fundamentals in this book are not limited to select types of synthesizers or those from a particular company, but apply to most all hardware and software synthesizers that have evolved since the mid-1960s.

My First Synthesizer

I began programming synthesizers as a teenager, when my parents gave me a Roland SH-2000 (see figure 1.1 next page) synthesizer on my sixteenth birthday. I didn't have a clue what all the knobs, sliders and switches on the left side panel did; but by moving them, I was able to learn that "when I move this, I get this sound." In other words, I would associate a sound with a specific physical movement.

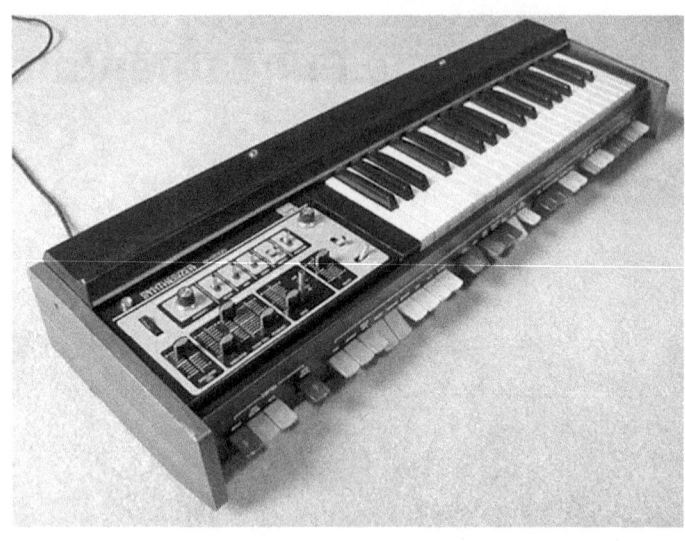

Figure 1.1 – A Roland SH-2000 (1973 – 1981)

At the time, I was the keyboard player for a rock band and began to combine the synthesizer with electronic keyboards (electric piano, organ, etc.). Playing spacey intros and synth melodies for our concerts was creative and lots of fun! The SH-2000 had tabs along the front of the keyboard that recalled 30 different factory preset sounds. These sounds could be modified with the switches and knobs found on the left side panel, but the SH-2000 didn't have any function that would let me store my own sounds. I had to recreate the positions of the switches and knobs every time I wanted an original sound, thus I became a "programmer" very quickly from trial and error.

Over the following years, my skills with synthesizer programming grew as I purchased and learned to use more sophisticated synthesizers. Working as a professional musician, in time I acquired a Yamaha CS-40M, a Yamaha SK50D, a Moog Liberation, an Oberheim OB-Xa, and many others. With each synthesizer, I learned something new as I used them in bands on stage and in the studio.

While my skills improved, I programmed and played these instruments for years without any in-depth understanding of how they work. When I became an electronic music composition major at the University of Tennessee, I began to acquire the theory behind what all those knobs and sliders were doing. It was a great education and I really enjoyed using my newfound knowledge. Now, I could quickly learn to program or tweak sounds on most any synthesizer, and get exactly the sound I needed.

You can do the same! Learning the fundamentals in this book will give you the ability to quickly understand a range of both hardware synthesizers, from companies such as Yamaha, Roland, Korg and Moog, and software synthesizers from companies such as Native Instruments, Spectrasonics and Reason Studios. Are you ready? Let's go!

Sounds vs. Patches: The Modular Synthesizer

When you work with synths, you'll often hear sounds referred to as "patches." This term comes from the method used to create a sound with early modular synthesizers.

The first commercial synthesizers were built in the 1960s by instrument designers such as Bob Moog and Donald Buchla. These synthesizers were comprised of various hardware modules that were mounted in a case and then connected together by patch cables. Figure 1.2 shows Bob Moog with one of his early modular synthesizers.

Figure 1.2 – Bob Moog and a Modular Synthesizer

The idea was that you could connect most any module to any other in really creative ways. As you can see, the programmer had myriad choices for connecting modules. Typically, a signal was routed out of one module and into another; in other words, one end of a patch cable was connected to an output while the other was connected to an input. Once the programmer had plugged in a few patch cables and all related controls (knobs and switches) were set, a sound was created that could be played via a connected keyboard or other controller. Since you had to patch together modules to create a sound, synthesizer programmers and players began to refer to sounds as "patches."

Technology at the time didn't allow a patch to be stored for later recall (a common feature on today's synthesizers). Repatching and reprogramming was necessary each and every time a different sound was desired. This made it essential to understand synthesis fundamentals when using one of these instruments.

With most modern synthesizers, patch cables and programming are not required. Nevertheless, the basic architecture of these synthesizers is the same as it was on the first modular synthesizers built in the 1960s. That's why learning how these modular synthesizers worked provides the basis for understanding how most any synthesizer works – and why this book takes a modular approach to learning synthesis.

Since about 1970, most synthesizers, both hardware and software, have been designed in a way to avoid the need for patch cables. Rather, the connections for signals are hardwired "under the hood" to provide the most useful, common configurations. In other words, signals between modules are "normaled" with little, if any, choices for changing them. While this is less flexible than true patching, it makes programming much quicker and easier.

Figure 1.3 – A Moog Voyager and Reason's Subtractor

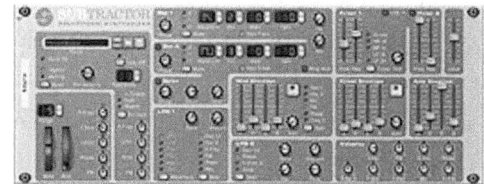

Examples of modern synthesizers that use this approach are shown in figure 1.3. On the left is a hardware analog synthesizer known as the Moog Voyager; on the right is a software synthesizer known as Subtractor (included in the Reason virtual workstation). Notice how their panels – both real and virtual – are divided into separate sections. These sections are analogous to the modules found in a modular synthesizer.

Since the various sections are interconnected for you, to create a sound all you have to do is set the various controls (knobs, sliders and switches) until you are satisfied with your "patch." These modern synthesizers have patch memory, so you can store your patch for later recall without the need to reprogram for each sound.

This Book Covers Subtractive Synthesis

The majority of synthesizers (including the ones we have already discussed) are based on a technology called "subtractive synthesis," which can be defined as a type of synthesis in which a sound is created by taking a waveform (sound source) rich in harmonics and using a filter to "subtract" harmonics to create new sounds. Since this is the predominant type of synthesis, it is the type covered in this book, and we'll look closely at how it works.

Although less common, there are other types of synthesis, such as frequency modulation, granular synthesis, and additive synthesis. Details about these types of synthesis are beyond the scope of this book.

Two Signal Types

Before proceeding to more complex topics, it is important to have an understanding of the two types of signals used in synthesizer modules: audio signals and control signals. An audio signal comprises the actual sound that you will eventually hear from the synthesizer's output. A control signal, in contrast, is not sound but an electronic signal that allows one module in a synthesizer to control some aspect of another module. For example, the keyboard of a synthesizer provides a control signal that affects the pitch of the audio signal, allowing you to play notes of specific pitches.

It is also important to make a distinction between control signals and MIDI, the Musical Instrument Digital Interface. MIDI is used to connect synthesizers, workstations, computers and other music gear to one another; a control signal is used to affect the parameters of modules within a given synthesizer. For my information on MIDI, see the book "The Fundamentals of MIDI".

Module Types

Synthesizer modules are divided into three types: source, modifier, and controller.

A *source* initiates an audio signal. The two most common sources are the oscillator and the noise generator (NG). An oscillator produces the basic pitched sound in a synthesizer. It is called an "oscillator" because it generates sounds that vary repetitively, or oscillate. Think of a string on a guitar. When you pluck it, it vibrates back and forth, or oscillates, at a rapid rate and produces sound. An electronic oscillator differs in that sound is produced electronically, and brought to the ear through an amplifier and speakers or headphones, rather than produced mechanically.

A noise generator produces the basic unpitched sound on a synthesizer. If you listen to the output of a noise generator directly, with no processing at all, it sounds like the noise you hear between stations on an old AM radio.

A *modifier* receives and processes the audio signal from a source. The two most common modifiers are the filter and the amplifier. A filter on a synthesizer, in the most simple case, is a lot like a tone control on a boom box or home theater system: it will control the brightness of a sound as it is manipulated. Similarly, an amplifier on a synthesizer is a lot like a volume control: it will control the amplitude of a sound as it is manipulated. Unlike simple tone and volume controls, though, filters and amplifiers on a synthesizer can be controlled rapidly in complex ways, and form a big part of the character of a synthesizer's sound.

A *controller* controls the parameters of another module. The three most common controllers are the envelope generator (EG), low frequency oscillator (LFO), and a keyboard.

An *envelope generator* produces a specific type of control signal in response to a "trigger," or event. This control signal is produced only once per each trigger, and repeats for each new trigger. A common trigger source is depressing a key on a musical keyboard. An envelope generator signal is the equivalent of moving the knob on a tone or volume control, but occurs much more rapidly and provides a much more complex and subtle degree of control.

A *low frequency oscillator* is similar electronically to the audio oscillator, but oscillates very slowly (typically from once every few seconds to a several times a second). It is used to produce repetitive changes in sound; for example, setting the rate of an LFO to about three cycles per second and sending the output to the control input of an Oscillator will produce vibrato.

You will sometimes hear the oscillator, filter and amplifier referred to as the Voltage Controlled Oscillator (VCO), Voltage Controlled Filter (VCF), or Voltage Controlled Amplifier (VCA), respectively. This is old school terminology that relates to the type of technology used in vintage synthesizers to implement the control system, but the principals of programming synthesizer sounds are the same no matter which technology is used.

Figure 1.4 shows a simple block diagram of the three module types and the signals that connect them.

Figure 1.4 - A source, modifier and controller connected by audio and control signals

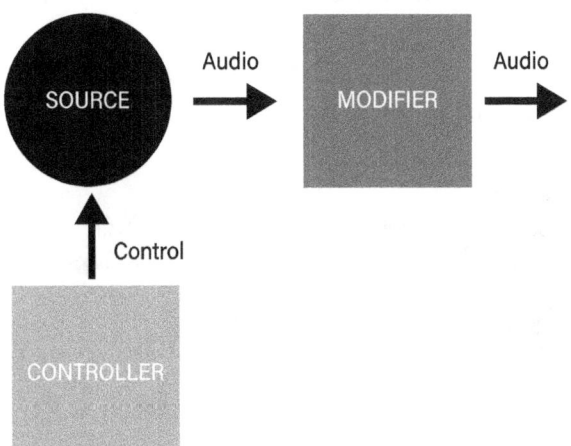

Notice that the source is in the upper left of the diagram with an audio signal drawn horizontally. In a block diagram, the audio signal is assumed to flow from a source to a modifier, generally from left to right in the diagram. Also notice the controller is placed beneath the source with the control signal drawn vertically. A control signal is assumed to flow from a controller to a source, generally from bottom to top in the diagram. Note that this is a highly simplified diagram as there would normally be multiple modifiers and controllers.

Input and Outputs

On a modular synthesizer, each jack is an input or an output for audio or control signals. Even though it is not necessary to use patch cables on most synthesizers today, it helps you to understand signal flow if you know the typical inputs and outputs found on the three module types.

Being the initiator of an audio path, a *source* type module has an audio output. Since *modifiers* process an audio signal, they must have both an audio input and output. *Controllers* do not have an audio input or output, but only a control output. All module types have control inputs. For the sake of clarity, this is demonstrated in the following table (figure 1.5).

Figure 1.5 – Inputs and outputs for sources, modifiers and controllers

Module Category	Input/Output
Source	audio output
Modifier	audio input and output
Controller	control output
All Three	control input

To recap, looking again at the previous figure 1.4, you see the source has an audio output, the modifier has an audio input and output, and the controller has a control output. The source is also using a control input.

Let's say your synthesizer has these three modules. Now that you know all modules have a control input, it should make sense to you if we took the control signal coming from the controller in figure 1.4 and re-routed it to the modifier like you see in figure 1.6. This would likely be done with a switch or selector on the front panel of your synthesizer.

Figure 1.6 – A control signal routed from a controller to a modifier

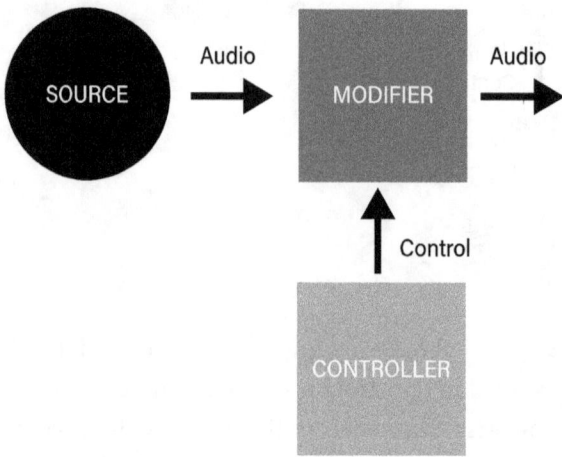

The Basic Model for Subtractive Synthesis

The basic model for subtractive synthesis builds on the concepts above. It is comprised of three modules that make up the audio path in a synthesizer: a source and two modifiers connected via two audio signals (figure 1.7). The source is an oscillator, and the modifiers are a filter and an amplifier (the controllers are discussed below). Most every synthesizer is built around this model. Memorize it before you continue reading.

Figure 1.7 - The basic model for subtractive synthesis

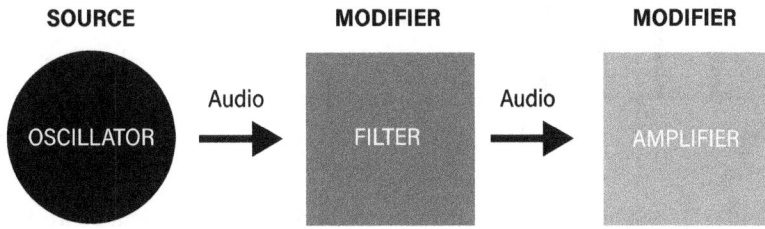

The Properties of Sound

Let's take a brief look at the properties of sound before continuing with synthesis. There are many books that go into great depth on this subject, but for the purpose of this book, we will just touch on the basics.

There is a relationship between the three modules in figure 1.7 and the three properties of sound: *pitch/frequency*, *timbre/spectrum*, and *loudness/amplitude*. *Pitch*, *timbre* and *loudness* are used within a musical context whereas *frequency*, *spectrum* and *amplitude* are used within a scientific context. You will see all these terms used in synthesis as the context requires.

Pitch and *frequency* are the "high" and "low" of a sound. For example, a violin plays notes that are high in pitch or frequency, while an upright bass plays notes that are low in pitch or frequency.

Pitch and *frequency* relate to the speed of oscillation of a sound-producing mechanical device or electronic circuit. When something oscillates, it fluctuates periodically between two points or levels. For example, a pendulum is a mechanical oscillator that swings back and forth from one side to the other.

Conventional musical instruments are also mechanical oscillators. When you pluck the highest string on a guitar, it oscillates back and forth at the rapid rate of 329.63 times per second. This is so fast that a moving guitar string is just a blur to the naked eye, but if you "slow down" the motion using a stroboscope, you can actually see the string move back and forth. Synthesizers generate sounds electronically, rather than with mechanical devices such as strings, but the general concepts of oscillation and *pitch/frequency* still apply.

In a musical context, as we noted, the speed of oscillation is referred to as "pitch" and is referenced as different notes that are given the letter names A through G. Looking at a musical keyboard, you can see that there are twelve different notes (i.e., keyboard keys) in sequence before the pattern of notes repeats (see figure 1.8). Each twelve-note sequence is referred to as an "octave." Within each octave you will have seven white keys, which correspond to the notes A through G, as mentioned, along with five black keys that correspond to sharps and flats. (In music theory, the five black keys have what are called "enharmonic names," i.e., C sharp and D flat are the same.)

Figure 1.8 – The keyboard

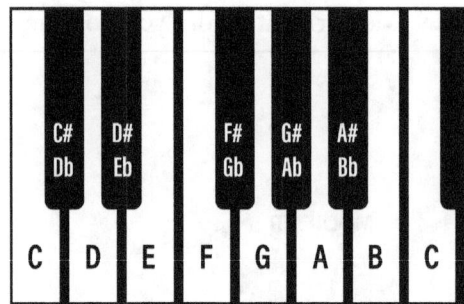

The distance from one note to another is called an interval. For example, the interval from one note to the very next one (e.g., from B to C, or from C to C#) is called a half-step or a *semitone*.

Pitches in between notes are important, too, as we'll examine in the next chapter. The distance from one note to another on a keyboard – one semitone – is divided into 100 equal parts called *cents*, i.e., 1 cent = 1/100 of a semitone. If a pitch falls between one of these notes, for example, if a vocalist sings a little low or high (e.g. 10 cents low or high), the vocalist is *flat* (below the correct pitch) or *sharp* (above the correct pitch).

In a scientific context, the speed of oscillation is referred to as "frequency" and is measured in units called *hertz* (named for the scientist Heinrich Hertz, and abbreviated Hz). A frequency of 1 Hz equals one oscillation per second. Musical oscillations cover a wide range of frequencies. The note you hear from the principal violinist when an orchestra tunes up is the A at 440 Hz, often called "concert A" (on a piano, this is the first A above middle C). The lowest note on a grand piano is at 27.5 Hz, while the highest note is at 4.186 kHz (kHz is the abbreviation for kilohertz, or one thousand hertz).

An important point is that the frequency exactly doubles for every octave; e.g., the note A one octave above concert A has a frequency of 880 Hz, while the note A one octave below has a frequency of 220 Hz.

Timbre (pronounced "tam - bur") is the tone quality of a sound. Timbre is a complex phenomenon and there is no simple measurement for it as there is with pitch/frequency; you will often hear timbre referred to with descriptive terms such as "dark," "bright," "metallic," or "warm."

Returning to our example of the guitar string, if you observe the entire plucked string under the light of a stroboscope, you'll see that its vibration is complex, consisting of many components. These components produce *harmonics*: additional parts of the sound that occur at integer multiples of the fundamental frequency.

In the case of a guitar, the harmonics would be the fundamental frequency (the frequency of the string as a whole) x 3, x 5, x 7, etc. These are referred to as the 3rd, 5th, 7th harmonics, etc.; the fundamental is referred to as the 1st harmonic. If the fundamental frequency = 200 Hz, the 3rd harmonic would = 600 Hz (3 times the fundamental frequency and the 5th harmonic would = 1 khz (5 times the fundamental frequency). Note, the term, *overtone*, is interchangeable with *harmonic* but is one number lower. For instance, the first overtone is the second harmonic (it is over the fundamental).

The harmonic content of acoustical instrument oscillations is not only complex but *dynamic*, meaning that it changes over time. Oscillations in a synthesizer, in contrast, are created electronically and though they may also have many harmonics, the harmonics are of a regular, predictable nature. In fact, they are so regular that when the most commonly used synthesizer oscillations are charted on graph paper, they form simple geometric shapes such as a sine curve, a triangle, a square, and a ramp or "sawtooth." The sounds from these common oscillations are easily recognized, as well, and synthesizer programmers often refer to them by the shape or form of the associated sound wave, i.e., the "waveform." We will explore sine, triangle, square, and sawtooth waveforms in detail in chapter two.

Loudness relates to how loud or soft sound is. In a musical context, terms such as "piano" (Italian for soft) and "forté" (Italian for loud) refer to loudness. You will see dynamic markings in sheet music abbreviated as *p* for piano or *f* for forte. In a scientific context, amplitude is measured in decibels (abbreviated as dB). For example, a very quiet sound might measure 20 db, while the threshold of pain for human hearing is 120 dB.

Relating the properties of sound to the modules in the basic model for subtractive synthesis is a good starting place for understanding the audio path of a synthesizer (see figure 1.9). Generally speaking, if you want to change the pitch/frequency, go to the oscillator. If you want to adjust the timbre/spectrum, adjust the filter. Finally, if you want to control the loudness/amplitude, control the amplifier.

Figure 1.9 - Basic model for subtractive synthesis and how it relates to the three properties of sound

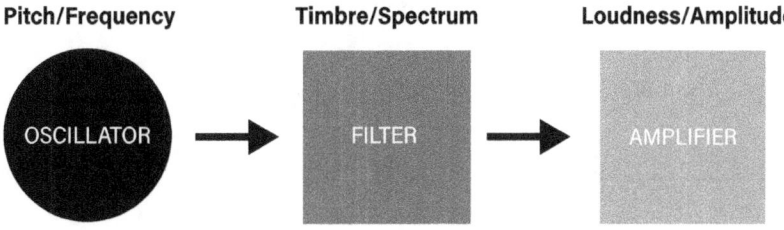

Summary

To summarize, this chapter introduced the basic architecture of a synthesizer, it's two signal types and three module types. The basic model for subtractive synthesis was introduced, and how each block relates to the properties of sound was discussed.

The following chapters will look at each module type in more detail. But first, answer the questions on the next page to test your understanding of this chapter.

Questions for Chapter 1

1. When you work with synths, you'll often hear sounds referred to as _____. This term comes from the method used to create a sound with early _____ synthesizers.

2. Which is a type of synthesis in which a sound is created by taking a waveform rich in harmonics and using a filter to "subtract" unwanted harmonics?
   a. additive synthesis
   b. subtractive synthesis
   c. frequency modulation
   d. granular synthesis

3. The two types of signals used in synthesizer modules are _____ and _____.

4. A _____ module initiates an audio signal.

5. A _____ module will receive and process an audio signal from the source.

6. A _____ controls the parameters of another module.

7. A(n) _____ produces a specific type of control signal in response to a "trigger," or event.

8. Source modules have a(n) _____ output, modifier modules have a(n) _____ input and output, controllers have a(n) _____ output.

9. The three properties of sound are _____ / _____, _____ / _____, and _____ / _____.

10. With a fundamental of 200Hz, the third harmonic will be _____ Hz.

11. If you want to change the pitch/frequency for a synthesizer, go to the _____.

12. In the space below, draw a block diagram of the basic model for subtractive synthesis (three blocks). Label inside the 3 blocks and draw and define the 2 signals. Also add the three properties of sound, showing how they relate.

T W O

Sources

This chapter is divided into nine sections:
1. Introduction
2. The Oscillator
3. Oscillator Controls for Pitch
4. Oscillator Controls for Harmonic Content
5. Noise Generator
6. Combining Waveforms
7. Advanced Oscillator Functions
8. Summary
9. Questions for Chapter Two

Introduction

As described in chapter one, a source module is the start of the audio signal path. It's the audio signal that eventually makes its way to your ears. Without at least one source, no sound can be created with a synthesizer. That would be like having a guitar with no strings!

As you've learned, the two types of sources commonly found on a modular synthesizer are the oscillator and the noise generator. The rest of this chapter covers those modules in detail. You will learn about the most common controls (knobs, sliders, switches, etc.) associated with the oscillator and noise generator. While these controls may vary somewhat (especially the names) from one synth to another, they are all based on the same concepts. Let's begin with the oscillator.

The Oscillator

The dictionary says an oscillator is "a device for generating oscillating electric currents or voltages by non-mechanical means." What does oscillating mean? When something oscillates, it fluctuates periodically between two things. For instance, a pendulum is a mechanical oscillator that swings back and forth from one side to the other. Differently, an electronic oscillator generates a repetitive electronic signal in the form of a periodic waveform. The periodic waveform will represent a specific pitch (frequency) and shape (timbre).

A synthesizer typically has one, two or three oscillators. At minimum, each one has controls – either physical controls on a panel, or virtual controls in software – that allow you to adjust the pitch and waveform coming from its audio output. The pitch of each oscillator is typically also controlled by playing a musical keyboard, but for now we will focus on the basic oscillator controls.

Oscillator Controls for Pitch

Let's begin our discussion with controls that are responsible for adjusting pitch. We will call these *fine tune*, *coarse tune*, and *octave selector*. As previously mentioned, each of these controls is found as either a hardware or virtual slider or knob on the "front panel" (which itself could be a hardware or virtual panel) of the synth. However, different synths may have different names for them, and in some cases a synth may not have all three controls or may combine two of them in a unique way. Let's discuss each pitch control in detail.

Fine Tune (sometimes labeled "detune") allows you to adjust the pitch of an oscillator by very small intervals over a short range. As you move the control, the pitch will change in discreet steps of cents (1/100th of a half-step), typically over the range of a half or whole step. For example, while sounding the note A3, manipulating the fine tune control would allow you to adjust the pitch 50 cents higher (half way to A#3) or 50 cents lower (half way to G#3). This allows you to make very fine changes to pitch and get in-between notes.

Coarse Tune will allow you to adjust the oscillator pitch by larger intervals over a wider range. As you move the control, the pitch will typically change in discreet steps of semitones (half-steps) over a range of one or more octaves. For example, while sounding the note A3, manipulating the coarse tune control will typically allow you to change pitch 12 steps higher (to A4) or 12 steps lower (to A2). This allows the pitch for an oscillator to be quickly changed to a musical interval such as a major third or a perfect fifth. (Note that on many true analog synthesizers, the control knob or slider will change fine and coarse tune smoothly and continuously, not in discreet steps.)

The *octave selector* allows you to change the pitch of an oscillator quickly by octaves. Moving this control changes pitch in discreet steps over a range of four, five or more octaves. For example, an octave selector will allow you to move an A3 up to A4 or A5, or down to A2 or A1, without changing the adjustment of the coarse and fine tune controls. This allows you to quickly set the pitch range of your instrument. For example, lower settings would be more appropriate for a bass patch where higher settings would be appropriate for a lead patch.

Figure 2.1 summarizes the three typical pitch controls of an oscillator.

Figure 2.1 – The pitch controls for an oscillator

Control	Interval	Range
Fine Tune	Changes pitch by cents	Half or whole step
Course Tune	Changes pitch by semitones	One to several octaves
Octave Selector	Changes pitch by octaves	Four or more octaves

Figure 2.2 shows the oscillators from two different synthesizers, Subtractor (from Reason Studio's Virtual Workstation known as Reason) and a Moog Voyager (a hardware analog synthesizer from Moog Music). Both are given here for comparison (no two synths are the same). Notice Subtractor has two oscillators (labeled Osc 1 and Osc 2) and the Voyager has three (labeled 1, 2 and 3). Notice all the various knobs and switches are labeled differently. However, they are very similar in concept.

Figure 2.2 – The oscillators from Subtractor and the Voyager

Subtractor (in figure 2.2) has three controls that correlate with the three controls previously described as fine tune, course tune and octave switch. The control labeled "Cent" is the fine tune control. Clicking the up/down arrows will change pitch in discreet steps by cents over a range of a semitone (-50 to +50). The next small window to the left, labeled "Semi", is the course tune control. Clicking the up/down arrows will change pitch in discreet steps by semitones over a range of one octave (0 to 12 with no negative numbers). The next small window to the left, labeled "Oct", is the octave selector. Clicking the up/down arrows will change pitch in discreet steps by octaves over a range of 10 octaves (0 to 9).

The Voyager is different. Notice oscillators two and three each have a knob labeled "Frequency". This control allows you to change pitch smoothly up and down by a perfect fifth. This knob is not necessarily a fine tune or course tune control as previously defined, but rather a combination of the two. Its range is a little over an octave (like course tuning) but it also allows you to do fine tuning with subtle movements in the knob. This is possible since pitch is changed smoothly (and not in discreet steps) on an analog synthesizer.

The control labeled "Octave" on the Voyager is exactly like octave selector as previously defined. Notice it can select 6 different octaves: 32, 16, 8, 4, 2 and 1.

Oscillator Controls for Harmonic Content

An oscillator provides a specific pitch but also provide specific harmonic content (timbre) through various waveforms. Two oscillator controls affect the waveform: *waveform selector* and *pulse width*.

We touched on waveforms in chapter one. A waveform is defined as "a graph showing the shape of a wave at a given time." As you learned, synthesizer waveforms, if viewed with time slowed down, have very regular, geometric shapes that give the waveforms their names. Each different waveform has different harmonic content and, therefore, a different timbre.

There are five common shapes (waveforms) found on analog synthesizers: *sine, triangle, square, sawtooth* and *pulse*. The *waveform selector* allows you to select one of these five waveforms. Let's discuss these common waveforms in more detail.

The *sine wave*, also referred to as a pure tone, contains the fundamental frequency only. In other words, it includes just the first harmonic. For example, a sine wave with a fundamental of 100 Hz will generate only a 100 Hz tone with no additional harmonics. It has a simple, pure sound. Figure 2.3 shows one cycle of a sine wave, as viewed on an oscilloscope, and its associated harmonic content (fundamental only).

Figure 2.3 - A sine wave as viewed on an oscilloscope and its harmonic content

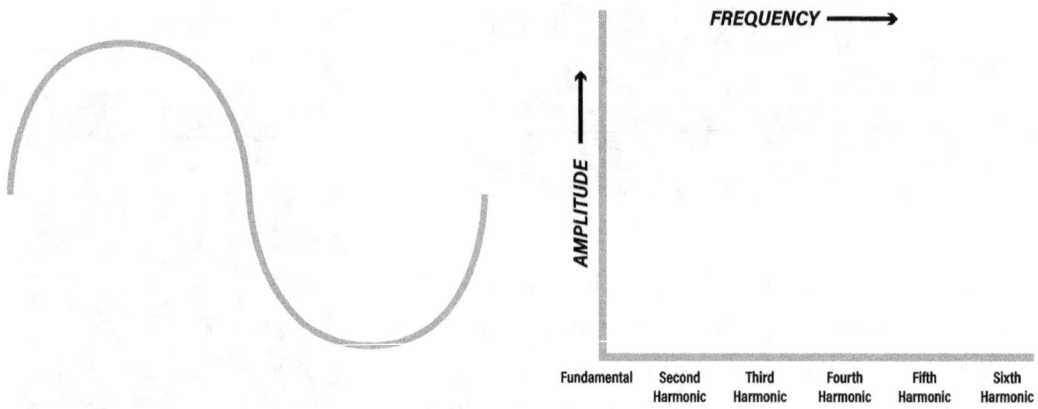

The *triangle wave* has odd harmonics only (3rd, 5th, 7th, etc.). For example, a triangle wave with a fundamental at 100 Hz will also have harmonics at 300 Hz, 500 Hz, etc. The relative amplitude of each harmonic in a triangle wave is given by the formula $1/n^2$, where "n" is the number of the harmonic. In figure 2.4, the 3rd harmonic at 300 Hz would have a relative amplitude 1/9 that of the fundamental, the 5th harmonic at 500 Hz would have a relative amplitude 1/25 that of the fundamental, etc. These harmonics cause the triangle wave to sound slighter brighter, fuller and louder than the sine wave.

Figure 2.4 – A triangle wave as viewed on an oscilloscope and its harmonic content

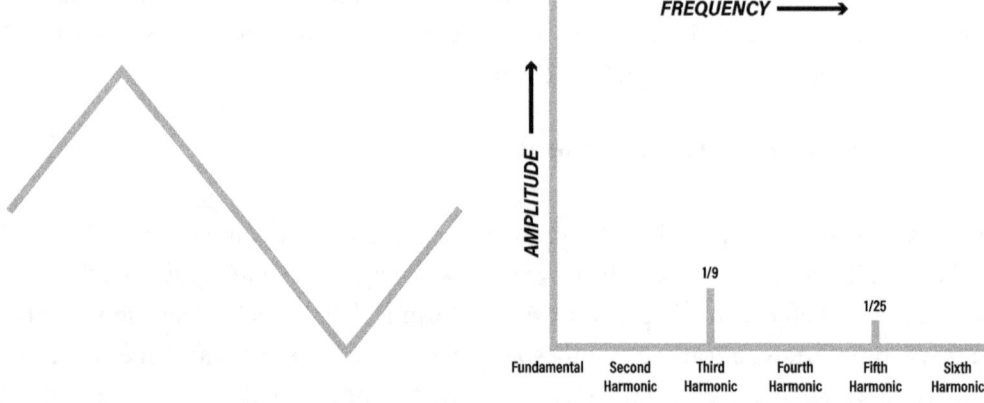

The *square wave*, like the triangle wave, has odd harmonics only. However, the relative amplitudes of the harmonics are greater. The relative amplitude of each harmonic in a square wave is given by the formula $1/n$. The 3rd harmonic would have a relative amplitude 1/3 that of the fundamental, the 5th harmonic would have a relative amplitude 1/5 that of the fundamental, etc. These stronger harmonics cause the square wave to sound brighter and louder than the triangle wave (see figure 2.5).

Figure 2.5 – A square wave as viewed on an oscilloscope and its harmonic content

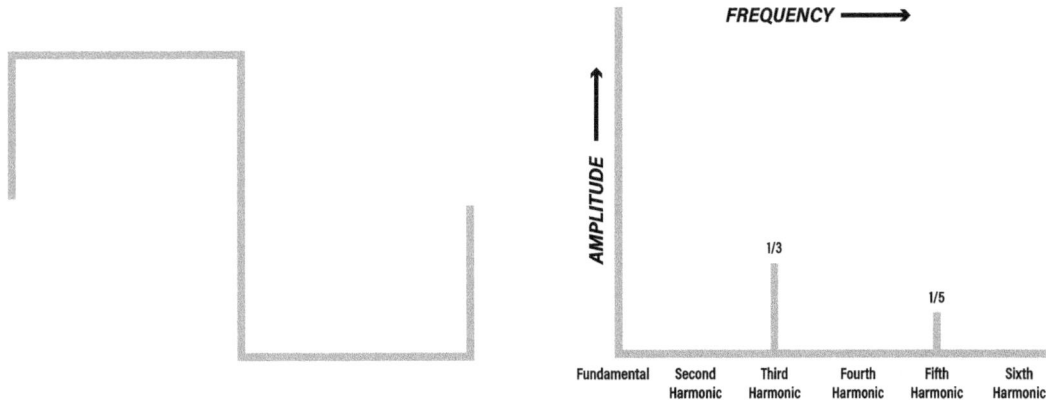

The *sawtooth wave* has all harmonics, odd and even. For example, a sawtooth wave with a fundamental at 100 Hz will also generate harmonic frequencies at 200 Hz, 300 Hz, 400 Hz, 500 Hz, etc. As with the square wave, the relative amplitude of each harmonic in a sawtooth wave is given by the formula 1/n. The amplitude of the 2nd, 3rd, 4th and 5th harmonics are 1/2, 1/3rd, 1/4th and 1/5th the amplitude of the fundamental, respectively. These added harmonics cause the sawtooth wave to sound bright and buzzy (see figure 2.6).

Figure 2.6 – A sawtooth wave as viewed on an oscilloscope and its harmonic content

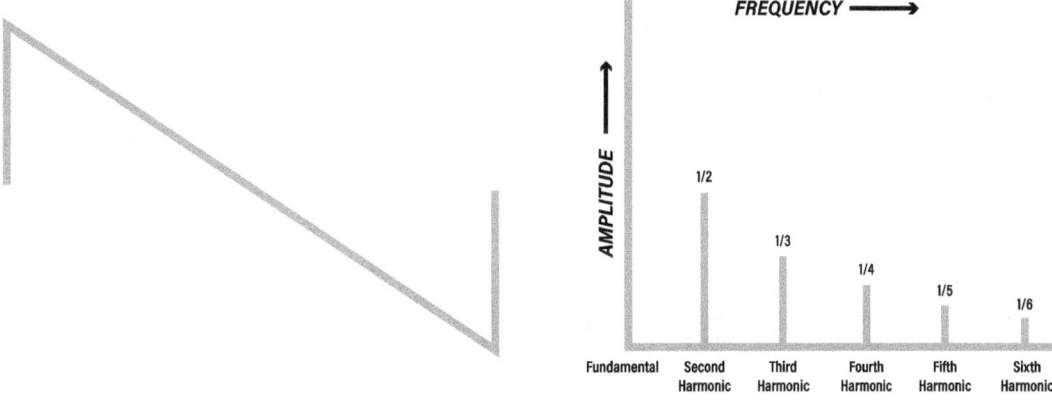

The *pulse wave* shape, unlike that of other waveforms, is variable. The shape and harmonic content of the pulse wave can be changed using the *pulse width* control. In technical terms, adjusting the pulse width control allows you to change the "duty cycle" of the pulse wave, or the relative time that the waveform is "on" during one complete cycle. For example, a square wave has a pulse width of 50% (1/2) of the cycle (see figure 2.5 again).

Changing the pulse width changes the harmonics in predictable ways. For example, if the pulse width is reduced to 25% (1/4) of the cycle, the harmonic content would change so that every 4th harmonic is missing. In other words, the harmonics would include the 2nd, 3rd, 5th, 6th, etc. (see figure 2.7). For another example, if the pulse width is 1/5th (20%), every 5th harmonic would be missing. The harmonics would include the 2nd, 3rd, 4th, 6th, etc.

The Fundamentals of Synthesizer Programming

Figure 2.7 – A pulse wave with a pulse width of 25% (1/4)

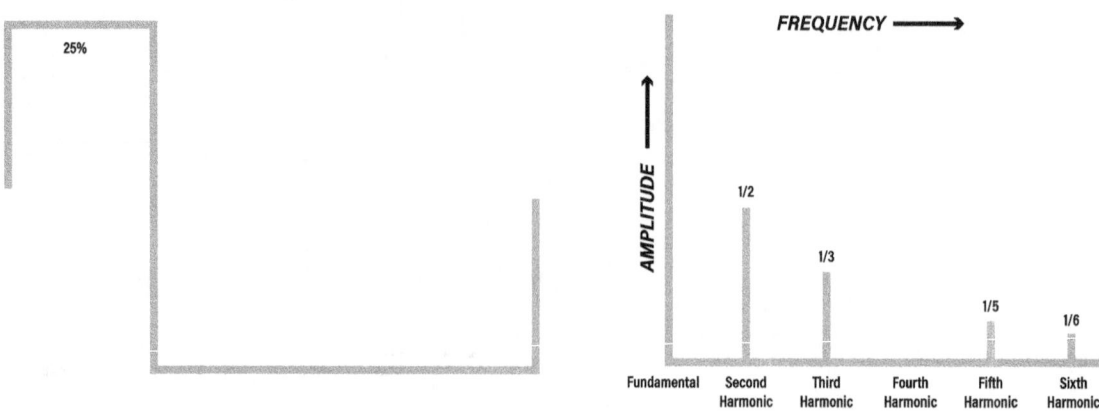

The pulse width control allows you to smoothly change the pulse width resulting in many different timbres from a single waveform. This becomes even more interesting when a controller such as a Low Frequency Oscillator (LFO) affects the pulse width. This is referred to as Pulse Width Modulation and causes a single oscillator to have a "thicker" sound that varies at the rate of the LFO. LFO control will be discussed further in chapter five.

Note that some synthesizers allow you to change the shape of all waveforms. This type of control may have a different name, such as "symmetry" or "phase." Looking at Osc 1 in Subtractor (figure 2.8), the small window labeled *Waveform* is the waveform selector. Clicking the up/down arrows will allow you to select different waveforms. The knob farthest to the left, labeled *Phase*, allows you to apply pulse-width-like control to *any* selected waveform (the "X" or "-" mode must be first selected).

Figure 2.8 – An oscillator on Subtractor

In comparison, figure 2.9 shows the wave selector for the Voyager. Notice only four different waveforms are available. However, the knob to select them is continuous allowing you to morph from one waveform to another. This allows you to fall in between the four waveforms. There is no pulse-width control.

It is helpful to learn the harmonic content of each waveform, but it is imperative that you listen to all the waveforms from a synthesizer and know how they sound. It would be an additional help to listen to waveforms from many synths and to view them through an oscilloscope. Figure 2.10 summarizes the five waveforms and their harmonic content.

Figure 2.9 – The wave selector on a Moog Voyager

Figure 2.10 – The five common waveforms found on a synthesizer

	Harmonic Content of Waveforms
Sine	Fundamental only
Triangle	Odd harmonics only
Square	Odd harmonics only
Sawtooth	All harmonics
Pulse	Harmonics determined by the pulse width (duty cycle)

While analog synthesizers from the '60s and '70s were limited to the five basic waveforms, most synths developed since include many more. For example, Subtractor includes four of the five basic waveforms and 28 more "special" waveforms. They are labeled by a number from the panel but are further described in the Reason manual. In comparison, the Yamaha Motif XS, a hardware digital keyboard workstation, has 2,670 waveforms! In contrast to the waveforms from an analog synth, the waveforms on the Motif XS are digitized samples (recordings). Many are recognizable instruments such as the piano, guitar, etc. Selecting one of these waveforms will allow you to create a patch that comes much closer to imitating one of these instruments.

Noise Generator (NG)

The *noise generator* (NG) is a source that is very different from the oscillator. It generates a random signal that includes all frequencies. It does not produce a specific pitch or timbre that would be used for musical melodies and harmonies, rather it produces noise that is ideal for creating percussion sounds or special effects such as wind, thunder, ocean waves, helicopters, etc.

Compared to an oscillator, there are far fewer controls provided for a noise generator, in some cases merely a level control; however, many synthesizers allow you to choose a noise "color." Noise color refers to the overall spectrum of the noise. White noise and pink noise are the most common. White noise contains equal energy per bandwidth while pink noise contains equal energy per octave. For example, with white noise, the energy between 100 Hz and 200 Hz is the same as between 1,100 and 1,200 Hz (because they both equal the same bandwidth). With pink noise, the energy between 100 Hz and 200 Hz is the same as between 1,000 Hz and 2,000 Hz (because they both equal one octave). With pink noise, amplitude increases as frequency increases. Put simply, white and pink noise sound different. Experimentation is probably the best way to become familiar with the noise generator.

Figure 2.11 shows the Noise module found on Subtractor. The little box in the upper left corner simply switches noise on or off. The knob labeled "Color" allows you to gradually change between pink and white noise. (The knob labeled Decay allows you to apply an envelope. Envelopes will be discussed further in chapter five.)

In comparison, the noise generator on the Moog Voyager simply has an on/off switch and a level control (see figure 2.12).

Figure 2.11 – The NG on Subtractor

Figure 2.12 – The NG on the Moog Voyager

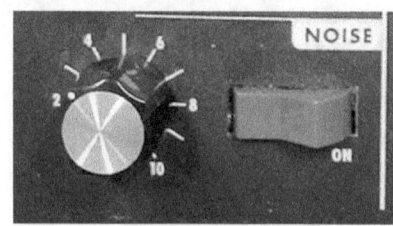

Combining Waveforms

Most synthesizers incorporate multiple sources, such as two, three or more oscillators and a noise generator. This allows the programmer to come up with complex patches by combining these sources and setting the available controls for each source to different parameters. For example, in figure 2.13 you see that Subtractor provides two oscillators (labeled Osc 1 and Osc 2) and a noise generator.

Figure 2.13 – Available sources on Subtractor

Most synthesizers allow some method of switching your sources on/off. Notice in figure 2.13 that Osc 2 is activated (highlighted) and Noise is muted via tiny boxes in the upper left corners.

Some method of balancing the amplitude levels of your sources should be provided. Figure 2.14 shows a block diagram of a mixer and two oscillators. The mixer should have controls that allow you to adjust the amplitude level of each oscillator resulting in a mix. This configuration is analogous to using a mixer to adjust the levels coming from multiple instruments.

Figure 2.14 – A block diagram of two oscillators and a mixer

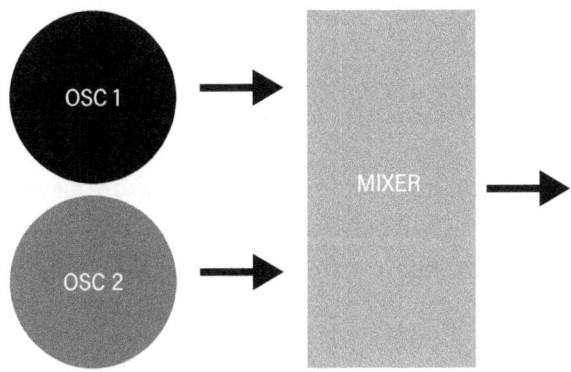

This block diagram transfers easily to the Voyager. Notice in figure 2.15 that the mixer section on the front panel shows five different sources, each with an on/off switch and a level control. Notice the first source is labeled "External". Some synthesizers have an audio input that allows an external device such as an mp3 player or an electric guitar to be used as a source. This can create some interesting effects when the external source is processed by a filter and amplifier, which we will discuss in the next chapter.

Figure 2.15 – The mixer section on a Moog Voyager

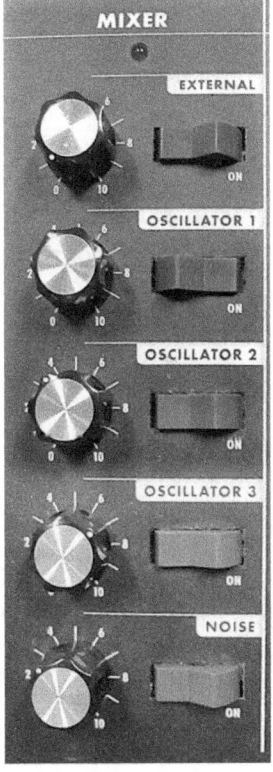

Looking at Subtractor again in figure 2.13, a single knob labeled *Mix* is used to balance amplitude levels between sources. Moving the Mix knob to the left or right balances between Osc 1 (to the left), and Osc 2 and the NG (to the right). The NG also has its on control for amplitude level (notice the knob labeled Level in the Noise section).

In addition to setting different levels, adjusting the previously discussed oscillator pitch controls to different parameters can yield a more complex patch. For example, using the fine tune control to detune two oscillators a few hertz apart will result in a thicker, more animated sound that has a periodic fluctuation in loudness referred to as "beating." Beating will occur at a rate that equals the frequency difference between the two oscillators. For example, if the frequency of one oscillator is 401 Hz and that of a second oscillator is 400 Hz, the rate of beating will be 1 Hz (401 - 400 = 1). If the first oscillator is raised to 403 Hz, the rate of beating becomes 3 Hz (403 - 400 = 3). Either way, your patch will sound fatter with beating, though faster beats can sound discordant.

A common practice is to adjust the fine tune control of one oscillator down a few cents and a second oscillator up a few cents. Figure 2.16 shows Osc 1 for Subtractor fine tuned 3 cents up and the other 3 cents down. Technically, this is no different than fine-tuning one oscillator up (or down) 6 cents and leaving the other oscillator fine tuned to 0, so you may wonder why this is done. On some synths, a third oscillator is provided (such as with the Voyager). If a third oscillator with fine-tuning at 0 is added to the two, there will be beating among all three, giving a very rich sound.

Figure 2.16 – Oscillators fine tuned for beating

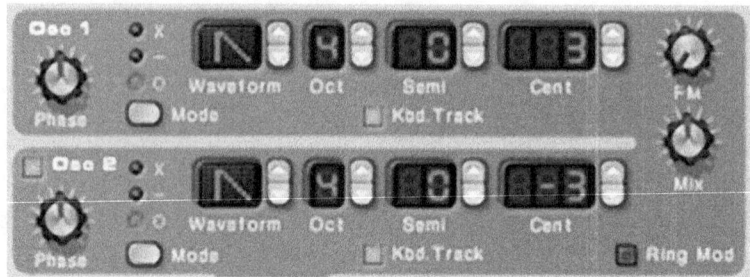

Note that the rate of beating between two detuned oscillators will change as higher or lower notes are played from a keyboard or other controller. For example, the rate of beating will halve when a note is sounded one octave lower, and double when a note is sounded one octave higher (figure 2.17). You should take this into consideration as you program patches that incorporate beating.

Figure 2.17 – Beating between two oscillators one octave apart

	Original Note	One Octave Higher
Osc 1 Frequency	400 Hz	800 Hz
Osc 2 Frequency	404 Hz	808 Hz
Rate of Beating	4 beats per second	8 beats per second

The oscillator course tuning controls can also be adjusted to produce more interesting sounds. For example, setting two oscillators seven half steps apart will result in an interval of a perfect fifth. When a melody or riff is played, you will hear parallel fifths (see figure 2.18). This combination is often heard in synth lead parts.

Figure 2.18 – Oscillators coarse tuned for parallel fifths

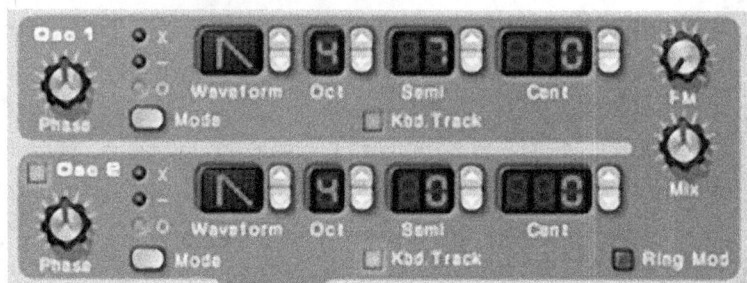

Finally, the octave switch for each oscillator can be set to different octaves. Setting oscillators to one, two or more octaves apart will result in interesting combinations. For example, this might be used to create an organ-like patch by stacking octaves, to "fatten" a bass patch by adding a lower octave, or to give the illusion of separate voices by tuning two oscillators several octaves apart.

Remember that in addition to different pitch settings per oscillator, you can have different waveform settings, too. Rather than setting each oscillator to the same waveform, try setting them to very different waveforms. Combining two different waveforms will create a totally new sound. Figure 2.19 shows two oscillators set to different waveforms and octaves.

Figure 2.19 – Oscillators set to different waveforms and different octaves

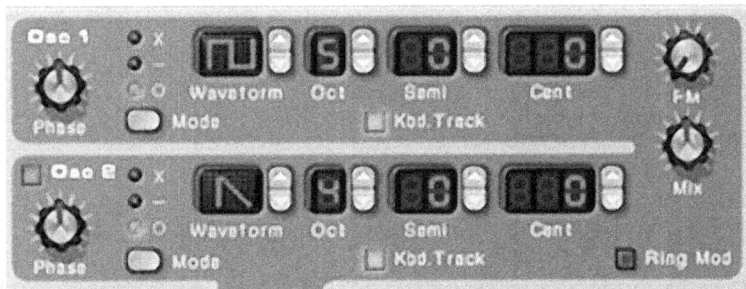

Advanced Oscillator Functions

Many modern synthesizers provide additional functions for changing oscillator timbre. Three common and important methods are hard sync, ring modulation, and frequency modulation.

Hard sync allows you to change timbre by "syncing" two oscillators. This forces one oscillator to restart its cycle in synchronization with the start of the other oscillator's cycle. Switching hard sync on doesn't sound all that interesting when the relative pitches of the two oscillators are static, but if you change the pitch of the sync'd oscillator with a pitch bend wheel or other controller while holding down a key, it produces an animated, vocal-like quality. This is recognizable in the song "Let's Go", a hit by The Cars from the 1980s. Figure 2.20 shows the Sync switch on the Moog Voyager. Switching it on will sync together oscillators 1 and 2.

Ring modulation combines the frequencies from two oscillators to produce a new audio signal that contains only the sum and difference frequencies of the two original frequencies (see figure 2.21). For example, if the two oscillators in figure 2.21 were producing sine waves at 250 Hz and 600 Hz, respectively, the output of the ring modulator would be sine waves at 850 Hz (the sum) and 350 Hz (the difference).

Figure 2.20 – The Sync switch on the Voyager

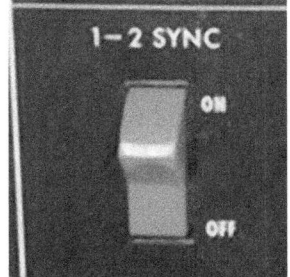

Figure 2.21 – Two oscillators and a ring modulator

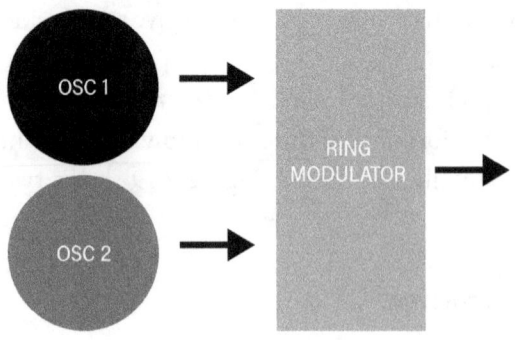

This can produce very metallic, bell-like timbres since the harmonics may no longer be integer multiples of the fundamental. Even more complex results can be accomplished if the oscillator waveforms have complex harmonic content (i.e., are not sine waves).

On some synths, a ring modulator is a separate modifier module; on others, it is a function added to the Oscillators. Figure 2.22 shows the ring modulator in Subtractor, which is simply a virtual on/off switch in the bottom right corner, labeled Ring Mod. Switching it to "on" passes the oscillator signals through the ring modulator.

Figure 2.22 – Ring modulation with Subtractor

For interesting results, try setting the oscillator coarse tune controls to wider intervals. Also, try disconnecting keyboard control from one of the oscillators (this is typically achieved by switching off "Kbd Track" or a similarly labeled function).

Frequency modulation (FM), like ring modulation, requires two oscillators. With FM, one oscillator, called the modulator, becomes the control signal for the other oscillator, called the carrier. In this case, only the output of the carrier is sent to the audio chain (see figure 2.23).

Figure 2.23 – FM with two oscillators.

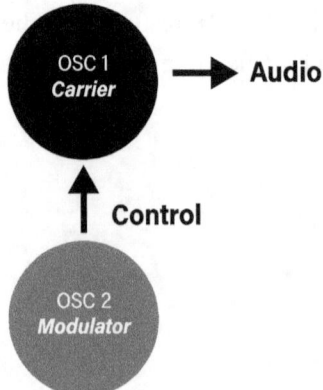

The audio output from the carrier (Osc 1) will include not only its frequency components but also complex sideband frequencies above and below that frequency. FM sideband frequencies are the sums and differences of the carrier and modulator frequencies multiplied by the "sideband number." For example, figure 2.24 shows the result of a carrier set to a sine wave at 500 Hz and the modulator set to a sine wave at 100 Hz. The first sidebands are 400 Hz (500 - (100 x 1)) and 600 Hz (500 + (100 x 1)). The second sidebands are 300 Hz (500 - (100 x 2)) and 700 Hz (500 + (100 x 2)).

Figure 2.24 - The carrier frequency (500Hz) and sidebands

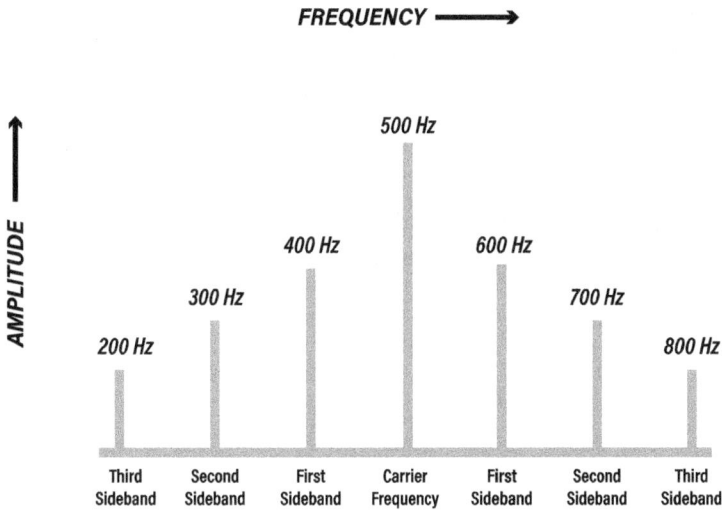

Also notice in figure 2.24 that as the sidebands move further from the carrier frequency, their amplitude decreases. There will typically be a control on your synth labeled *FM Amount* (or a similar label) that allows you to adjust sidebands. Increasing the amount will increase the amplitude and number of sidebands.

FM, even more than ring modulation, can produce very complex, bell-like tones where the harmonics are not integer multiples of the fundamental. Still more complex tones can be created if the waveforms include harmonic content.

Figure 2.25 shows the FM control knob in Subtractor, in the upper right corner of the oscillator panel. By turning this knob to the right, you are essentially rerouting the output of Osc 2 to function as a control signal to Osc 1. You will want to be sure that the Mix knob is turned all the way to the left (or you will also hear the Osc 2 output), and Osc 2 is switched on. Increasing the FM knob will increase the number of sidebands and their amplitude. Experiment with the coarse tuning (Semi) of Osc 2 to get many different, complex timbres.

Figure 2.25 - FM with Subtractor

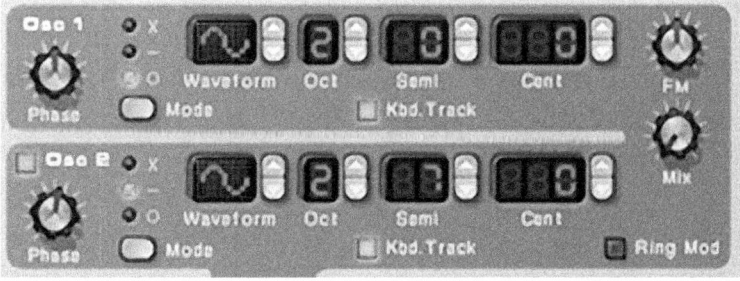

Summary

This chapter covered sources, their many controls, and different ways to combine them. By now you should have a basic working knowledge of sources, but it is essential that you practice programming so that you reinforce these fundamentals and hear what they do. Try reverse engineering some of the factory patches that come with your synthesizer. Load them in and look at what the programmer did. This is a great way to become more skilled at programming.

The next chapter will explain how the audio signal from a source is modified with a filter and amplifier, but first test your knowledge by completing the questions on the next page.

Questions for Chapter 2

1. The two types of sources commonly found on a synthesizer are a(n) _____ and a _____.

2. The three typical pitch controls found on the front panel of an oscillator are: _____, _____ and _____.

3. Fill in the blanks:

Control	Interval	Range
Fine Tune	Changes pitch by_____	Half or whole step
Course Tune	Changes pitch by_____	One to several octaves
Octave Selector	Changes pitch by_____	Four or more octaves

4. The _____ wave, also referred to as a pure tone, includes only the fundamental frequency.

5. The _____ wave and _____ wave have odd harmonics only.

6. The _____ wave includes all harmonics.

7. If the pulse width of a pulse wave was shortened to 20% (1/5) of the cycle, the harmonic content would change so that every _____ harmonic is missing.

8. A _____ generator generates a random signal that includes all frequencies.

9. _____ noise contains equal energy per bandwidth while _____ noise contains equal energy per octave.

10. A periodic fluctuation in loudness caused by slightly detuning two oscillators is referred to as _____.

11. If the frequency of one oscillator is 200Hz and a second oscillator is 202Hz, the rate of beating will be _____ cycle(s) per second.

12. Setting two oscillators seven half steps apart will result in an interval of a perfect _____.

13. If two oscillators passing through a ring modulator were producing sine waves at 350Hz and 600 Hz, the output of the ring modulator would be _____Hz and _____Hz.

14. With FM, a carrier oscillator is set to a sine wave at 600Hz and a modulator oscillator is set to a sine wave at 50Hz. The first sidebands will be _____Hz and _____Hz. The second sidebands will be _____Hz and _____Hz.

THREE

Modifiers

This chapter is divided into nine sections:
1. Introduction
2. The Filter
3. Filter Types
4. Filter Cutoff & Center Frequencies
5. Filter Slope
6. Filter Resonance
7. The Amplifier
8. Summary
9. Questions for Chapter Three

Introduction

As described in chapter one, a modifier receives and processes the audio signal from a source. Modifiers are in the audio path (recall the basic model for subtractive synthesis from chapter one). Without modifiers, you would be left with the unprocessed audio signal coming from your source(s), being unable to make any changes to it. Modifiers have a huge effect on your patches.

There are two common types of modifiers found on a synthesizer: the *filter* and the *amplifier*. These modules are covered in detail in this chapter. As in the last chapter on sources, you will learn the most common controls used in the filter and amplifier sections found on most synthesizers. Remember, from one synthesizer to another, these controls may vary (especially the names). However, they are all based on the same concepts. Let's begin with the filter.

The Filter

An electronic filter is "a circuit or device that passes certain frequencies and blocks others." Just like a coffee filter blocks coffee grains from getting in your coffee cup, a synthesizer filter blocks certain frequencies from the audio signal. To be more specific, the filter controls will allow you to block (filter) specific harmonics from the harmonic content of your source(s). This is where the term "subtractive synthesis" comes from: using a filter to block or "subtract" harmonic content generated by the source(s).

Most every synthesizer has at least one filter (some instruments have two with a variety of ways to configure them) that will have manual controls to allow you to shape the basic timbre. The four most common controls are: *filter type*, *slope*, *cutoff frequency*, and *resonance*. Again, these controls are not identical on every synth, but the basic concepts are the same.

Filter Types

There are four common filter types, referred to by names that describe their functions: *the low pass filter*, *high pass filter*, *band pass filter*, and *band reject filter*. As its name implies, the low pass filter passes low frequencies while filtering high frequencies; the high pass filter passes high frequencies while filtering low frequencies; the band pass filter will pass a specific band of frequencies; while the band reject filter will reject (block) a specific band of frequencies.

So, it is easy to remember the function of a filter by its name. A filter may be limited to one of these types or it may have a switch that allows you to select among multiple types. The latter is often referred to as a "multimode filter." Let's talk about each filter type in more detail.

The low pass filter is by far the most common type. Many synthesizers have only a single, low pass filter; nonetheless, this type of filter is very versatile, as we'll see later in this book. Figure 3.1 shows the frequency-response curve for a low pass filter. On the graph, signal amplitude (vertical axis) is plotted against frequency (horizontal axis). Going from left to right on this graph, you see the amplitude of the filter's output is unchanged (staying at 0 dB) until it begins to decrease at a around 300 Hz; from that frequency up, the signal is gradually attenuated. In scientific terms, the bands beneath and above the slope are referred to as the "pass band" and "stop band," respectively.

Figure 3.1 – The frequency-response curve for a low pass filter

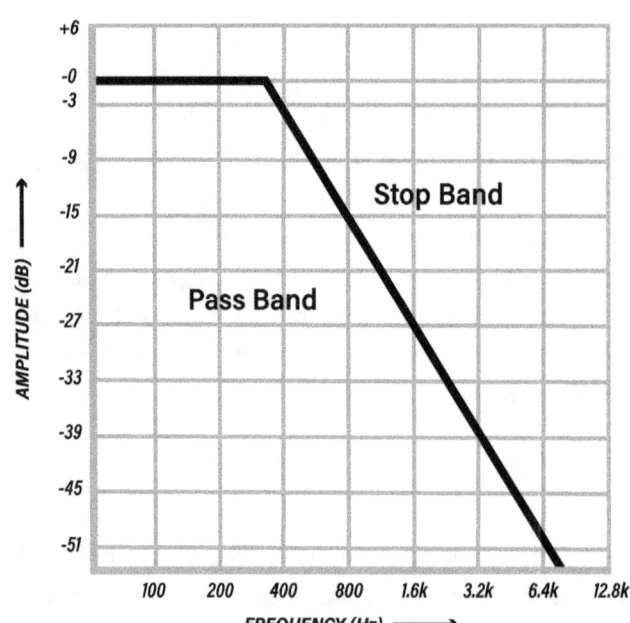

The second most common filter type is the high pass filter. Figure 3.2 shows the frequency-response curve for a high pass filter. As you can see, it is a mirror image of the low pass filter. Going from right to left in this case, the amplitude is unchanged until the amplitude begins to gradually drop off at about 2 kHz. It continues to drop off until complete attenuation is reached. All frequencies below this point are completely filtered (the stop band), and all frequencies to the right of the slope are passed (the pass band).

Figure 3.2 – The frequency-response curve for a high-pass filter

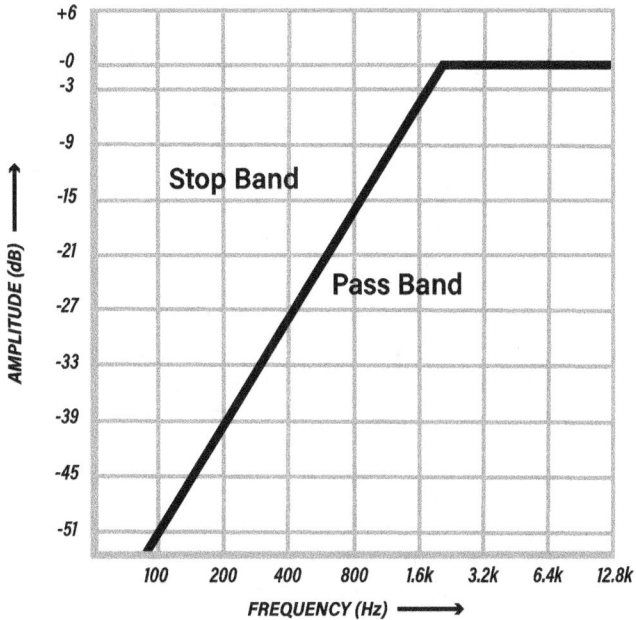

Figure 3.3 – The frequency-response curve for band-pass filter

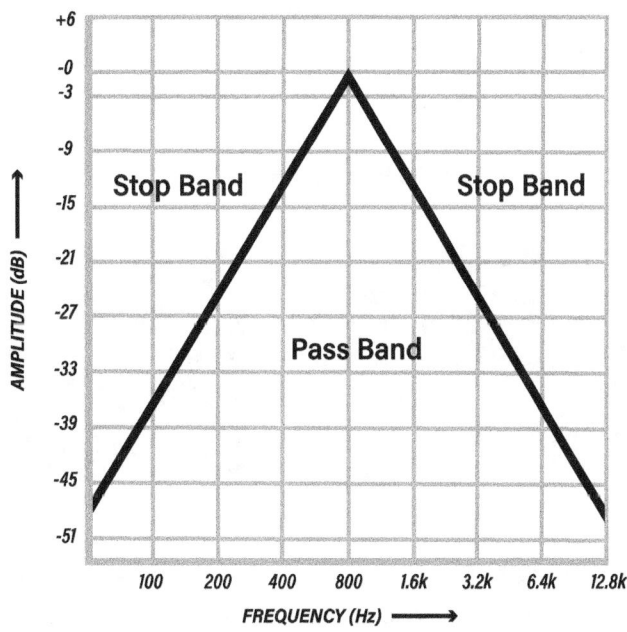

Two other, slightly less common filter types are the band pass and band reject filters. Figures 3.3 and 3.4 show the frequency response curves for each of these filters. The band pass filter will pass a specific frequency band while blocking frequencies below and above this band. Conversely, the band reject filter will reject a specific frequency band while passing frequencies below and above this band. Because of the shape of its output curve, the band reject filter is sometimes referred to as a "notch" filter.

Figure 3.4 – The frequency-response curve for a band reject filter

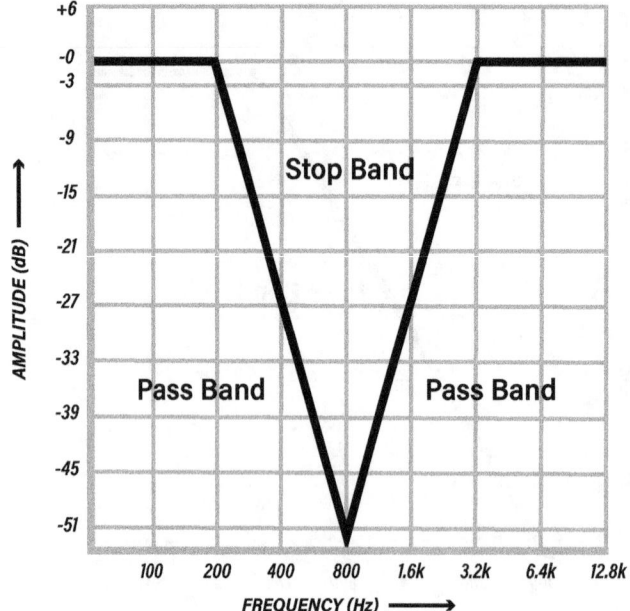

Let's take a look at Subtractor to see what types of filters it provides. In figure 3.5, you see that Subtractor has two filters (Filter 1 and Filter 2). Filter 1 is a multimode filter that allows you to select among two types of low pass (LP) filters, a band pass filter (BP), a high pass filter (HP), and a Notch (band reject) filter. (The numbers to the right of the filter type abbreviations describe the slope and will be explained later.) Filter 2 is strictly a low pass filter.

Figure 3.5 – The filters in Subtractor (L) and the Voyager (R)

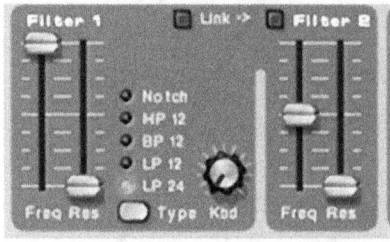 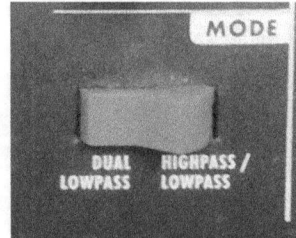

The Moog Voyager offers two choices: a low pass and a band pass. More specifically, it has two low pass filters that are connected in parallel allowing you to have a separate cutoff frequency for each audio output (more on cutoff frequency coming) and a high pass and low pass connected in series resulting in a band pass filter.

Filter Cutoff & Center Frequencies

Figure 3.6 shows the response curve of a low pass filter. Notice that the filter begins to attenuate just below 400 Hz and reaches an attenuation of -3 dB at 400 Hz. In scientific terms, the frequency at which a low pass filter (or high pass filter) achieves -3 dB of attenuation is called the cutoff frequency. This concept also applies to a high pass filter.

Figure 3.6 – The cutoff frequency for a low-pass filter

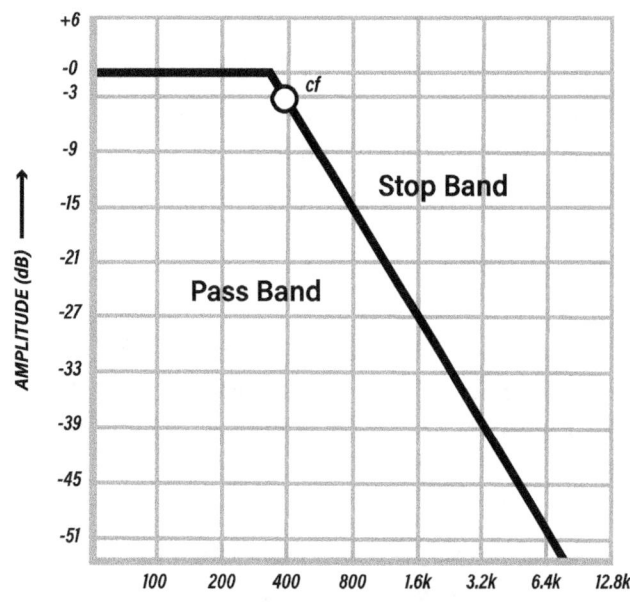

The cutoff frequency is manually controllable with a knob or slider. Typically, as you move this control from left to right (or from bottom to top) the cutoff frequency will sweep across the audio spectrum. This effect is something like a treble control on a home theater system, but is much more pronounced and the frequency range is much greater. Manipulating the cutoff in this way is referred to as a "filter sweep" and is a very common synth sound.

Looking again at figure 3.6, a full manual sweep of the cutoff frequency would start at the far left, blocking almost all frequencies, then gradually move to the right (toward the maximum cutoff frequency), until reaching the point where all frequencies are allowed to pass.

A manual filter sweep demonstrates the potential of this technique, but the most versatile implementation of a filter sweep uses either an envelope generator or an LFO to sweep the cutoff frequency. We'll explore this technique in detail in chapter four.

With band pass and band reject filters, we refer to the center frequency, rather than the cutoff frequency. For a band pass filter, the center frequency is defined as the frequency at which there is no attenuation. For a band reject ("notch") filter, the center frequency is defined as the frequency at which there is complete attenuation.

Looking back at figures 3.3 and 3.4, notice the center frequencies are at 800 Hz, meaning you have no attenuation or complete attenuation at this frequency depending on the filter mode you choose. Typically, the same manual control that allows you to change the cutoff frequency for low pass and high pass filter types will allow you to adjust the center frequency for the band pass and band reject filter types.

Looking again at the Voyager (figure 3.7), the cutoff frequency (or center frequency for band pass mode) is adjusted by the knob labeled *Cutoff*. The knob sweeps across the audio spectrum from left to right. Notice the cutoff is set close to 250 Hz. For a low pass filter, this means that frequencies below will be passed and frequencies above (to the right) will be blocked.

Figure 3.7 – The Cutoff frequency knob on the Voyager

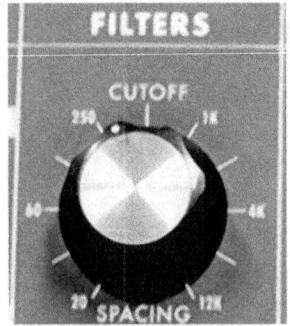

Try gradually moving the cutoff frequency on your synthesizer from minimum to maximum and back, and listen to the result. Try this with each filter type to help to understand their differences. Also try it with different sources (oscillator and noise).

Filter Slope

By now you will have noticed that the frequency-response curves of filters change gradually, creating a sloped shape on the graph. This is because attenuation occurs gradually and not abruptly. This shape is referred to as the filter slope, or "roll-off," and the steepness (the rate of attenuation) is not the same for every filter. In fact, some synths allow you to select different slopes for the same filter.

In scientific terms, slope is defined as the rate of attenuation per octave (in decibels). With low pass and high pass filters, two very common slopes are 12 dB per octave and 24 dB per octave. Figure 3.8 shows each of these slopes for a low pass filter.

Figure 3.8 – Slopes at 12dB and 24dB per octave for a low pass filter

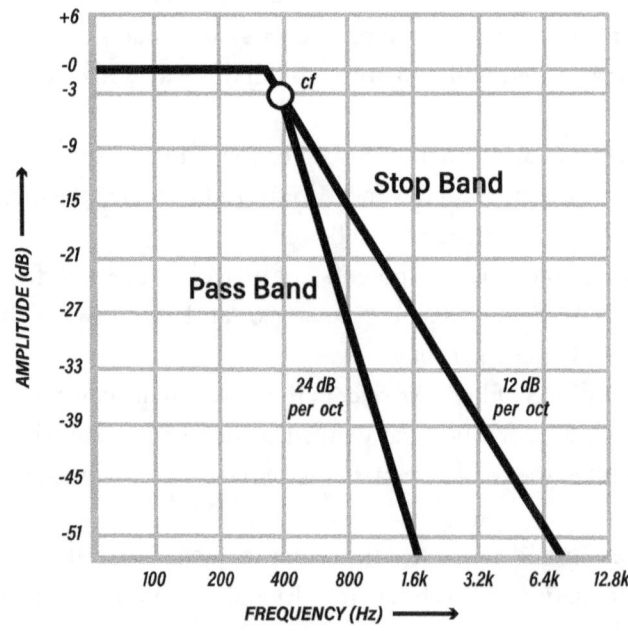

Notice in figure 3.8 that with a 12 dB per octave slope, the attenuation is -15 dB at one octave above the cutoff frequency. This is because the attenuation at the cutoff frequency is already -3 dB. Add 3 dB (the attenuation at the cutoff frequency) and 12 dB (the rate of attenuation) to get 15 dB (the amount of attenuation at one octave above the cutoff frequency). Similarly, in the case of a 24 dB per octave slope, the attenuation is -27 dB at one octave above the cutoff frequency.

These common slopes were established in classic analog synthesizers from the '60s. Moog synthesizers, including their modular synths and the famous Minimoog, used a 24 dB per octave low pass filter; while the competing Arp synthesizers, including their modular synths and the famous Odyssey, used a 12 dB per octave low pass filter. Moreover, the Moog filter was designed to be intentionally overdriven, if desired, while the Arp filter was designed to run clean. This gave vary different timbres from the two designs, the Moog filter sounding fat, aggressive, and slightly dark; the Arp filter sounding more open, clean, and bright.

You will occasionally see filters described by "poles," rather than slope. Poles refer to the number of stages in an electronic circuit used to build a filter. A 12 dB per octave filter is a "two pole" filter, whereas a 24 dB per octave filter is a "four pole" filter. Some synthesizers offer 6 dB per octave and 18 dB per octave slopes. These may be referred to as 1-pole and 3-pole, respectively.

Looking at the filters for Subtractor in figure 3.9, notice the numbers 12 and 24 next to the filter types (with *Notch* as the exception); these numbers indicate the slope. Subtractor's high pass and band pass selections are gentle 12 dB per octave slopes; for low pass, you can select between a gentle 12 dB per octave slope or a more aggressive 24 dB per octave slope. The notch filter does not have a selectable slope, but is affected by the resonance control, which we'll explore in the next section.

Figure 3.9 – The filters in Subtractor

Filter Resonance

So far, we have only discussed attenuation of the audio signal by various filter types, but you can apply amplification as well. This is achieved with the filter resonance control, which is sometimes called "emphasis," "feedback," or "Q" (for quality).

For a low pass or high pass filter, the resonance control will boost the source amplitude at the cutoff frequency. Figure 3.10 shows an example of resonance with a low pass filter. In this example, the cutoff frequency is set to 400 Hz and resonance is set to a high level.

You can see that in the case of the low pass filter, this creates a miniature "band pass" effect at the cutoff frequency, and that is how this effect sounds to the ear. In fact, with some low pass filters, high resonance creates a very pronounced "band pass" effect.

The resonance control is typically a knob or slider next to the cutoff frequency control. Referring again to figure 3.9, this is the slider labeled "Res" in Subtractor. When this control is set to minimum, no resonance is added. As you gradually add resonance, the response curve will become more and more like what you see in figure 3.10.

Figure 3.10 – A low pass filter with increased resonance

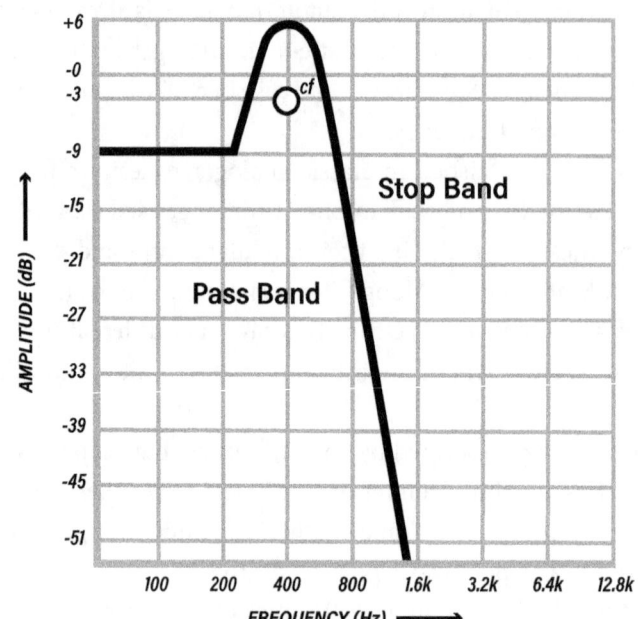

As mentioned previously, the band reject (notch) filter is an exception since increasing resonance decreases bandwidth (makes it more narrow).

Interestingly, with some filters if resonance is set to maximum the filter will self-oscillate. (This is true of the analog filters on Moog synthesizers, in particular.) This will sound like an additional sine wave at the cutoff frequency, added to the signal. Take care as you increase resonance as this can suddenly and greatly increase the output level -- and blow your speakers!

Sweeping the cutoff frequency control with the resonance set high will create those classic resonant synth-sweep sounds commonly heard with analog synthesizers. Using a low pass filter with resonance set near maximum (again, be careful when you adjust this as the level may increase suddenly), try manually moving the cutoff frequency very slowly through its range. You should be able to distinguish all the harmonics in your source waveform (choose different waveforms to compare their harmonic content).

The filter controls allow you to carve out frequencies from your sources, however, it gets much more interesting when you use controllers to modulate the filter, as we'll see in the next chapter.

The Amplifier

The amplifier is the second type of modifier. As with the filter, because of the prevalence of older technologies, it is sometimes referred to as the Voltage Controlled Amplifier (VCA).

In the audio path, the amplifier comes after the filter. In other words, the audio output of the filter connects to the audio input of the amplifier (recall the basic model for subtractive synthesis once more).

On a modular synthesizer, the only control an amplifier may have is a gain control that allows you to manually set the overall output level. The amplifier is not intended to be used alone but with a controller, typically an envelope generator. This allows the amplifier to shape the amplitude of a patch over time, which is critical to distinguishing sonically between sounds that sustain and sounds that decay, as we'll explore in detail in the next chapter.

Summary

This chapter covered modifiers and their controls. There are many controls for the filter but few or none for the amplifier. The next chapter will explain how sources and modifiers can be controlled by the third type of module, the controller.

Questions for Chapter 3

1. Circle the two types of modifiers found on a synthesizer.
    a. oscillator
    b. filter
    c. noise generator
    d. amplifier
    e. envelope generator

2. Which one is not a filter control?
    a. filter type
    b. cutoff frequency
    c. waveform selector
    d. filter resonance

3. A _____ _____ filter type has the stop band above the pass band.

4. A _____ _____ filter type has the pass band above the stop band.

5. A _____ _____ filter will pass a specific frequency band while blocking below and above this band.

6. A _____ _____ filter will filter a specific frequency band while passing below and above this band.

7. The _____ _____ is the frequency at which a low pass or high pass filter achieves -3 dB of attenuation

8. For a band pass filter, the _____ _____ is defined as the frequency at which there is no attenuation.

9. _____ is defined as the rate of attenuation per octave (in decibels).

10. A low-pass filter with an attenuation of 12 dB per octave with a cutoff frequency at 150 Hz will have an attenuation of _____ dB at 600 Hz.

11. A _____ dB per octave filter is a "two pole" filter, whereas a _____ dB per octave filter is a "four pole" filter.

12. For a low pass or high pass filter, the _____ control will boost the source amplitude at the cutoff frequency.

F O U R

Controllers

This chapter is divided into nine sections:
1. Introduction
2. The Filter
3. Filter Types
4. Filter Cutoff & Center Frequencies
5. Filter Slope
6. Filter Resonance
7. The Amplifier
8. Summary
9. Questions for Chapter Three

Introduction

The third type of module, the controller, was introduced in chapter one. You learned how controllers are used to affect parameters of source and modifier modules via control signals. Controllers are the key to more closely imitating acoustic instruments, adding expression to your sounds, making sound effects, and simply making patches more interesting.

Again, the primary purpose for a controller is to take control of another module via a control signal. The output of the controller is routed to the control input of one (or more) source or modifier modules.

You will see a range of terms used to describe controllers. For example, some synthesizers refer to a controller and modifier as a "source" and "destination," where the former is not really a "source" as defined in this book, but rather is the source of the control signal. Keep in mind that while the terminology may vary, the basic principles are the same.

Using a controller to affect a source or modifier is called modulation. A controller can modulate pitch, timbre or loudness depending on its destination (oscillator, filter or amplifier).

There are many types of controllers on a synthesizer. In this chapter, we will introduce the three most common controllers: the envelope generator, the low frequency oscillator, and the keyboard. Just like the last two chapters, you will learn the most common physical controls (knobs, sliders, switches, etc.) found on the front panel. However, it is also necessary to discuss routing since you will sometimes need to select a destination.

The Fundamentals of Synthesizer Programming

The Envelope Generator

In synthesis, an envelope refers to a control signal with a simple curve or shape that changes over time, based on values set by the programmer. Unlike oscillator waveforms, which change very quickly and are repetitive, envelopes can change over a period of many seconds — or even minutes — and do not repeat. The envelope generator (EG) is used to produce envelopes as control signals on a synthesizer.

Every musical instrument has both amplitude and timbral envelopes that are peculiar to that instrument. For example, when you play a note on a piano, you hear a very rapid rise in loudness that gradually decays as you hold down the key (or the sustain pedal). In contrast, when you play a note on an organ, you hear an instantaneous rise in loudness that sustains as long as you hold down the key.

With an envelope generator, you can recreate the envelopes of the piano, organ, or other conventional instruments. You can even create envelopes that don't resemble any known instruments.

When setting the envelopes for a new patch, you'll often start with the amplifier envelope to shape loudness. Typically, the amplifier will have a dedicated EG hardwired to its control input. Figure 4.1 shows a block diagram of this. Note that the signal from the EG to the amplifier is a control signal. Each time you press a key you will cause the EG to start.

Figure 4.1 – An EG routed to the amplifier with a control signal

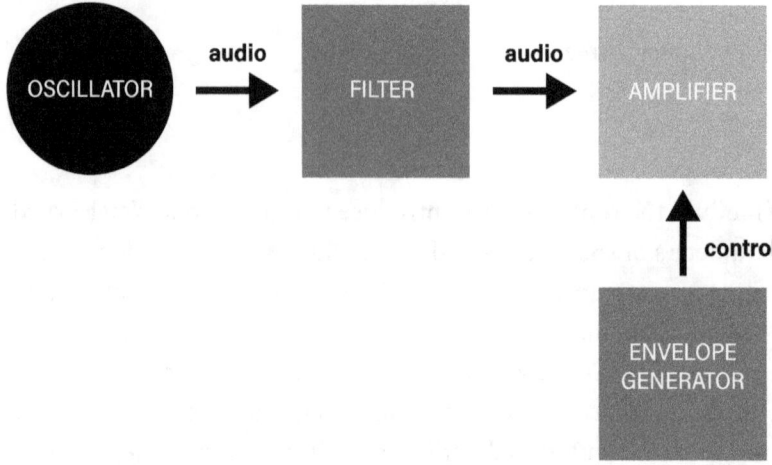

Every EG has multiple "stages" that determine how the envelope changes over time. By setting the controls for the various stages you can determine how quickly a sound starts, called "attack," how quickly a sound starts to die away, called "decay," whether or not a sound sustains while a key remains depressed, called "sustain," and whether the sound dies away gradually or stops after a key is released, called "release."

For convenience, the four EG stages are often abbreviated "ADSR" for Attack, Decay, Sustain, Release. It is helpful to think of the four stages as time, time, level, and time. The ADSR-type EG is the most common, but you will sometimes see synths that have more or fewer envelope stages. Let's discuss each of the ADSR stages for the amplifier in detail (we'll discuss the filter EG later in the chapter).

The *attack* stage determines the amount of time it takes for loudness to go from silence to maximum level. In other words, it determines the amount of time it takes for the sound to "build up" when you press a key. For example, you might set the attack time to zero for an organ sound, to a slightly slower rate for a guitar sound, or to a much slower rate for a string/pad sound. Attack times can range from a few milliseconds (a thousandth of a second) to many seconds, and different synths provide different minimum and maximum attack times. We will discuss the keyboard in more detail later, but this is a good time to point out that each time you press a key on a synthesizer's keyboard, the envelope generator is triggered to start. On an analog synthesizer, this is done with a gate signal (and possibly a trigger too) generated by the keyboard, but with a software synthesizer, this is accomplished with a MIDI Note-On message.

For example, with the attack stage set for two seconds, loudness will take this much time to gradually rise from silence to maximum each time a key is played (see figure 4.2). With all other subsequent stages (decay, sustain and release) set to zero, loudness will abruptly return to silence at two seconds.

Figure 4.2 – The attack stage from key on to maximum

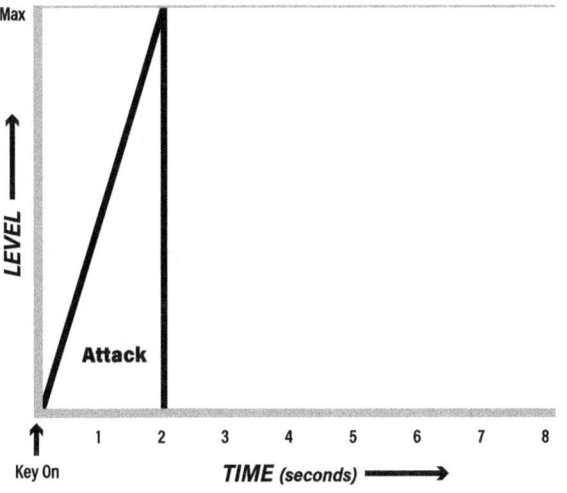

The *decay* stage determines how quickly the sound begins to die away after the attack stage is completed. Setting the decay value is somewhat more complicated, though, because the decay stage interacts with the *sustain* stage that follows it. A very important point to note is that the sustain setting reflects an amplitude *level*, not a time period. This is probably most easily explained by example.

In figure 4.3, the attack time is set for two seconds and the decay time is set for two seconds, as well; sustain is set to minimum level or zero. When you press a key and hold it, the sound will build up for two seconds, die away for two seconds, then become silent.

Figure 4.3 – Following the attack stage, loudness decays to a sustain level of 0

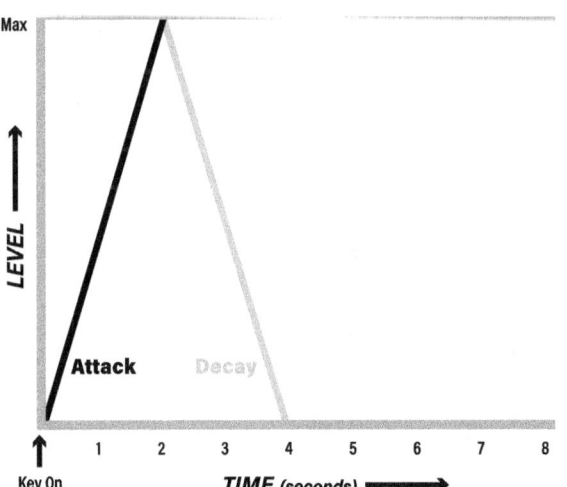

In figure 4.4, in contrast, the attack and decay times are still set for two seconds, but sustain is increased to 50%. Now, when you press a key and hold it, the sound will build up for two seconds, die away for two seconds, then continue to play at 50% amplitude until the key is released.

Figure 4.4 – Sound will remain at the sustain level until key off

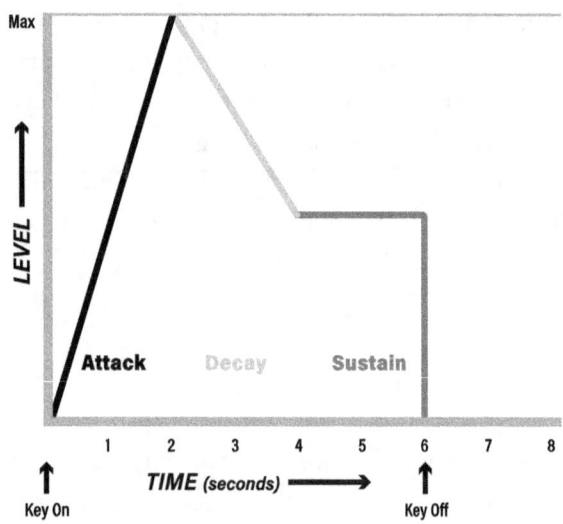

One point that is potentially confusing is that the decay stage is only active if the sustain level is set to less than 100%. In other words, the decay stage setting is irrelevant unless there is a sustain level below 100% to which it can decay.

The release stage determines the amount of time it takes for the sound to die away after a key is released. Keep in mind that the release stage will start when the key is released and the sound will die away from that level, which could be any level since it's possible for you to release the key during any of the previous three stages. Typically, though, the release stage starts after the sustain stage.

Figure 4.5 shows the release stage set for two seconds. Notice it is initiated after the key was held for six seconds.

As previously mentioned, a gate signal transmitted by a keyboard determines the start of the envelope. It also determines when the release stage begins. With a virtual instrument, this is accomplished with a MIDI Note-Off message (or a MIDI Note-On with a velocity of zero) transmitted from a MIDI keyboard controller.

Figure 4.5 – The release stage from sustain level to silence at key off

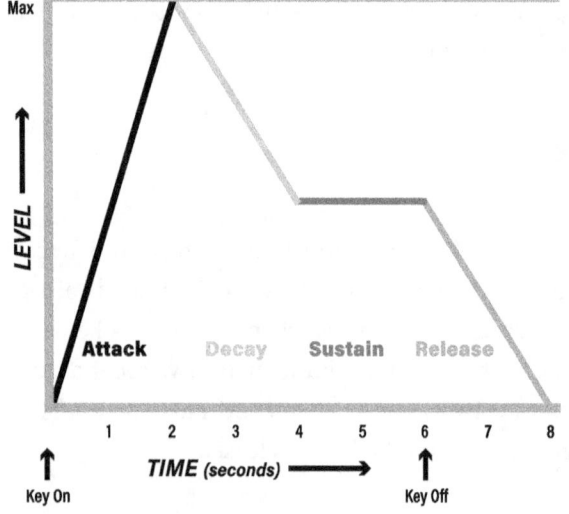

Remember, the sustain stage is a level setting while the other three stages are time settings. It helps to think of the four stages (attack, decay, sustain and release) as time, time, level, and time.

Figure 4.6 shows the amplifier envelope generator in Subtractor (labeled Amp Envelope). There is a slider for each stage with a range of 0 to 127.

Figure 4.6 – The envelope generator for loudness in Subtractor

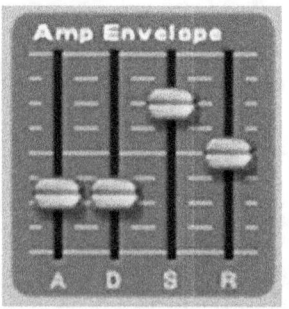

Figure 4.7 shows the amplifier envelope generator on the Voyager (labeled Volume). There is a knob for each stage with a range of 1 millisecond to 10 seconds.

Figure 4.7 – The envelope generator for loudness on a Voyager

The Filter EG

On most synths, an EG is also commonly dedicated to the filter. This is a powerful tool to control timbre. Figure 4.8 shows a block diagram of this common configuration. Notice there is an envelope generator for the filter and another for the amplifier. The former is optional but the latter is mandatory.

Figure 4.8 – EG's routed to the filter and the amplifier

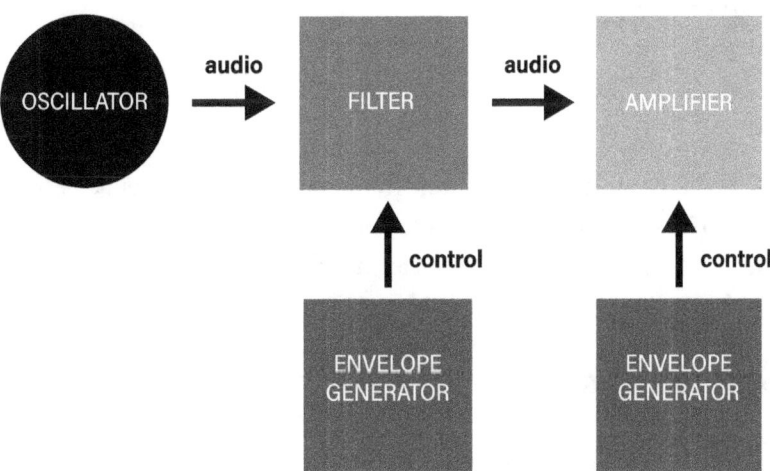

The filter EG will typically have the same stages (ADSR) and controls as the amplifier EG, however, the filter EG does not affect loudness, but instead controls the filter's cutoff frequency. In other words, the cutoff frequency will increase and decrease with time according to the envelope set by the ADSR controls.

Importantly, in addition to the standard ADSR controls, the filter EG has a control for the envelope "amount." The amount control can be thought of as a kind of "range" control for the filter EG, which adjusts how much effect the envelope has on the cutoff frequency without changing the settings or basic shape of the envelope. In other words, it does not affect the attack, decay, or release times, but does affect how high the cutoff frequency will go at the transition from the attack stage to the decay stage, and does affect how high the cutoff frequency is during the sustain stage. Let's see how these controls work together.

Figure 4.9 shows the envelope for a filter with the initial cutoff frequency set to 250 Hz and an amount control set so the cutoff frequency rises to 5 kHz. When a key is pressed and the envelope progresses, the cutoff frequency will increase at the attack rate, reaching a maximum frequency of 5 kHz at the transition from the attack stage to the decay stage, then decrease at the decay rate, remaining at the frequency determined by the sustain level until the key is released, at which time the cutoff with decrease at the release rate until it returns to the initial cutoff frequency of 250 Hz.

Figure 4.9 – An envelope for timbre change

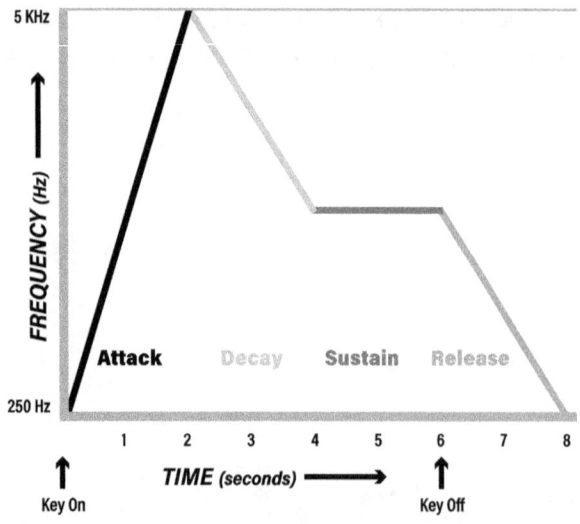

If the filter in figure 4.9 is a low pass type, more and more frequencies will pass as the cutoff frequency rises during the attack stage, making the sound progressively brighter; the opposite occurs if it is a high pass type. If the amount control is set lower, the cutoff frequency will not go as high. This would give less change in timbre, "darkening" the sound.

Figure 4.10 shows the filter envelope generator in Subtractor (labeled Filter Envelope). Notice the amount control in the bottom right corner (Amt). Subtractor also provides an additional EG control, the inverter switch in the upper right corner. This flips the envelope upside down, which can create some interesting effects.

When using a filter EG, be aware that your cutoff frequency control needs to be set to a frequency that allows the envelope to do its job. For instance, if the cutoff frequency is set too high, little or no effect will be heard from the filter. You typically want to set the cutoff frequency to a lower frequency (e.g. 250Hz) so you can hear it sweep the audio spectrum as it follows the envelope.

Figure 4.10 – The Filter Envelope in Subtractor

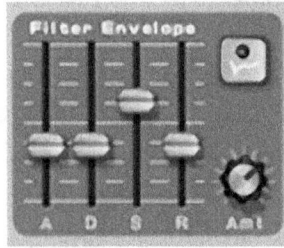

Also, be aware that changes to your filter EG may have no effect if the amplifier EG is not set to complementary values. For example, if the release stage on the amplifier EG is set to 0, changes to the release stage on the filter EG will be irrelevant as the sound will be inaudible during the release stage.

Other Uses for the EG

While dedicated envelope generators for filter and amplifier control are common on most all synthesizers, some synths have additional EGs or allow you to route an EG to other destinations, such as an oscillator control input. Figure 4.11 shows a block diagram for routing an EG to an oscillator. (Note that there must also be an EG for the amplifier.)

Figure 4.11 – An EG routed to the oscillator for pitch change

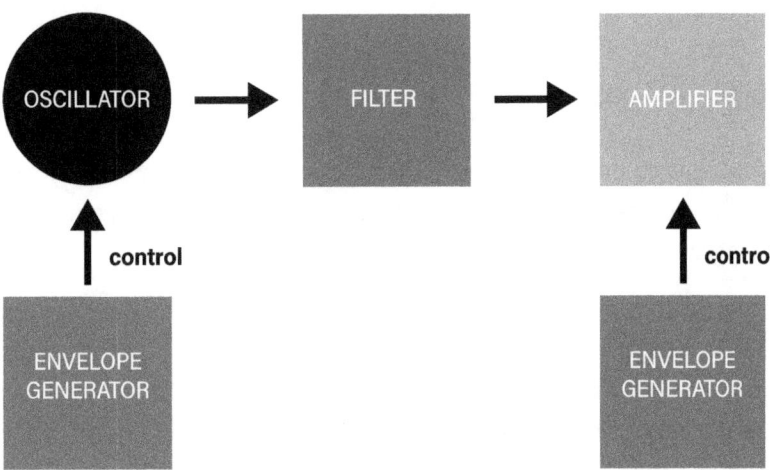

In this case, the oscillator pitch will follow the envelope, increasing from the oscillator's initial frequency value. The amount control will affect the range of the pitch change, in the same manner as it affects the cutoff frequency with a filter EG. In figure 4.12, pitch rises from 220 Hz to 3.52 kHz when pressing a key. When the key is released pitch will gradually return back to 220 Hz by the end of the release stage.

Figure 4.12 – Pitch follows the envelope shaped by an envelope generator

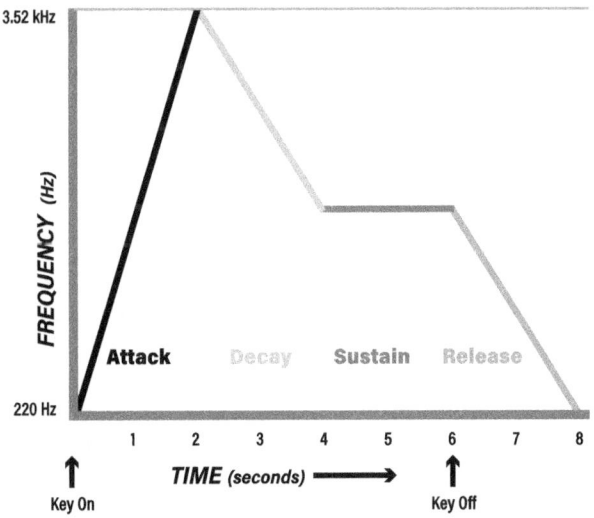

Looking at the Mod Envelope in Subtractor (see figure 4.13), you can see that it may be routed to a number of destinations, including the oscillators, second filter cutoff, and some rather esoteric functions. If the Amt control is set to zero, modulation is effectively "off."

The Fundamentals of Synthesizer Programming

Figure 4.13 – The Mod Envelope in Subtractor

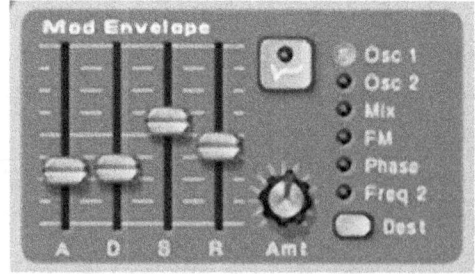

This type of EG control of a single oscillator can obtain a vocal-like timbre if used to control an oscillator that is sync'ed (recall Hard Sync from chapter two). Also, if with low amount settings, a quick attack/decay only envelope can be used to simulate the slight detuning that occurs when a string is plucked.

Single-Trigger vs. Multi-Trigger

As you've seen, a keyboard is commonly used to trigger an envelope generator. Many synthesizers allow you to determine how the envelope generators respond to repeated keystrokes by selecting either single-trigger or multi-trigger modes.

In *single-trigger* mode, the envelope generators will be triggered when a key is pressed, but will not be retriggered when other keys are pressed, until the first key is released. In other words, if you play a series of keys in a legato manner (smoothly connecting them without fully releasing), the EGs will simply continue the initial envelope for the entire series of keystrokes. The attack stage will not retrigger on each keystroke.

In *multi-trigger* mode, the envelope generators will retrigger the attack stage with every keystroke, whether previous keys have been released or not.

Figure 4.14 shows the envelope shape when two different keys are played successively and smoothly in single-trigger mode. As in figure 4.14, each key is pressed and held for three seconds. Notice that when the second key is pressed, the attack stage is not retriggered and the envelope remains at sustain level until it is released.

Except for special effects, it only makes sense to use single-trigger mode on a monophonic synthesizer or a polyphonic synthesizer with its polyphony set to 1 ("mono").

Figure 4.14 – Resulting envelope when two keys are played consecutively and smoothly with a single-trigger EG

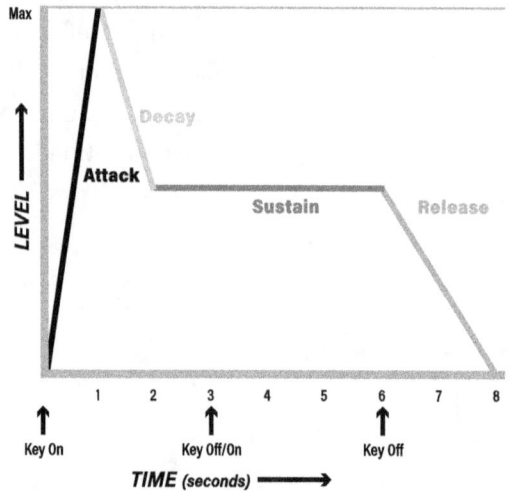

Figure 4.15 shows the envelope shape when two different keys are played successively and smoothly (legato) using multi-trigger mode. For this example, the attack and decay stages are set to one second each, and each key is pressed and held for three seconds. Notice that when the second key is pressed, the attack stage is retriggered.

Figure 4.15 – Same as figure 4.14 but with a multi-trigger EG

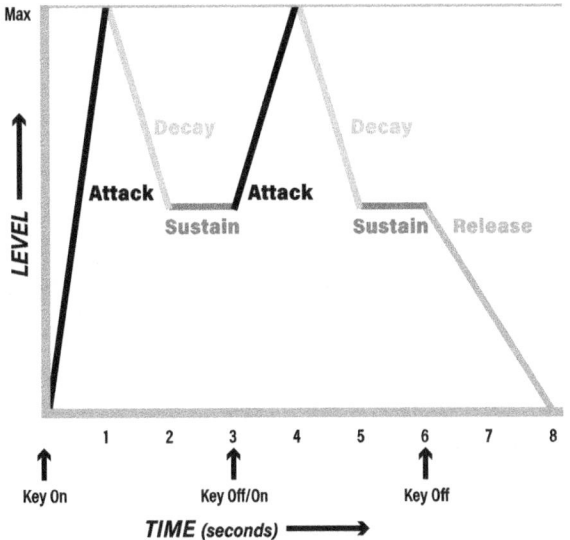

Figure 4.16 shows the single- and multi-trigger controls in Subtractor. Legato is equivalent to single-trigger mode and ReTrig is equivalent to multi-trigger mode.

Figure 4.16 – How to select the trigger mode for the EGs in Subtractor

The Low Frequency Oscillator

Another common and important controller is the low frequency oscillator (LFO). Unlike an oscillator used as an audio source, an LFO typically has a frequency range of less than 1 Hz to around 20 Hz. This is far below the range of human hearing but ideal for use in creating modulation effects.

Unlike the control signal from an EG, which progresses through its stages and then stops (or is retriggered), the control signal from an LFO is a true waveform that repeats continuously. In other words, when an LFO is used as a controller, pitch, timbre or loudness will change in a cyclical, repetitive manner and follow the shape of the LFO waveform. This is very useful for creating musical effects such as *vibrato* and *tremolo*, and for a myriad of special effects.

The LFO is routed to an oscillator, filter or amplifier, as desired. Figure 4.17 shows a block diagram of an LFO routed to an oscillator. On most synthesizers, this would be accomplished by assigning the LFO output to a destination labeled "oscillator," "pitch" or "frequency."

The Fundamentals of Synthesizer Programming

Figure 4.17 – An LFO controlling an oscillator

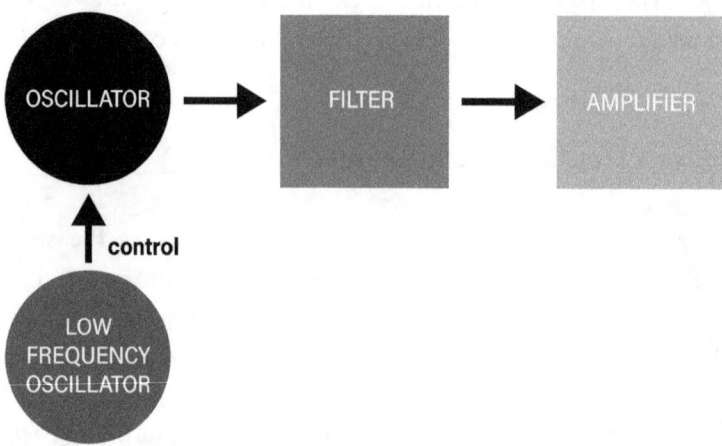

Obviously, this configuration will result in a change in pitch (frequency) and therefore may be referred to as pitch or frequency modulation. On many synths, the LFO may also be routed to other oscillator controls, such as pulse width or the second oscillator in a sync'd pair. As mentioned in chapter two, modulating the pulse width with a controller, which is called Pulse Width Modulation (PWM), is a great way to get a thicker sound from a single oscillator, and modulating one oscillator in a sync'd pair will produce interesting, vocal-like timbres.

If the LFO is routed to the filter, instead, the result will be a repeating change in timbre. This is referred to as filter or spectrum modulation. On most synthesizers, the destination is the cutoff frequency. In other words, the cutoff frequency for the filter will move across the audio spectrum as it follows the shape of the LFO waveform (think of automating the cutoff frequency). Some synthesizers also allow the filter resonance to be modulated.

If the LFO is routed to the amplifier, instead, the result will be a repeating change in amplitude. This is referred to as amplitude modulation and is used to create tremolo (a periodic variation in amplitude). In other words, the loudness of the amplifier will increase and decrease as it follows the shape of the LFO waveform.

On most synths, typical controls for the LFO include *frequency (rate)*, *waveform*, and *amount (depth)*. The frequency control is self-explanatory. As mentioned, the frequency range of an LFO is typically less than 1 Hz to about 20 Hz, but some synths can go much lower and much higher. A typical frequency setting for a vibrato effect might be about 3 to 5 Hz. Faster modulation frequencies will start to produce a "buzzing" sound, which is not representative of conventional vibrato, but can be useful for effects.

Figure 4.18 shows the frequency control on the Voyager labeled "Rate". Notice the range is from 0.2 to 50. The blinking light flashes at the set frequency.

Figure 4.18 – The frequency control on a Voyager

An LFO will typically provide fewer waveforms than an audio oscillator, but may include specialized waveforms that are suitable only for modulation. LFO waveform selection may be simplified, as well, with a group of simple buttons instead of a display with associated increment/decrement controls.

Common LFO waveforms include sine or triangle (less commonly, both are provided), square, sawtooth (ramp), reverse sawtooth (reverse ramp), and a complex waveform referred to as "sample and hold," which is discussed separately, below.

The LFO amount (or depth) control is similar to the amount control for an EG. For example, an LFO with a low amount setting routed to the control input of an audio oscillator will cause the pitch to change only slightly. Increasing the amount will cause pitch to change more and more noticeably (go higher and lower) over the period of the LFO waveform.

Figure 4.19 shows two cycles of an LFO with a square wave selected as its waveform. The first cycle has a low depth setting and the second cycle has a high depth setting. Imagine the pitch of the destination oscillator moving up and down to the shape of this waveform (a square wave). Obviously, pitch will go higher and lower for the second cycle. If the LFO were controlling the filter, the cutoff frequency would move to the shape of this waveform.

Figure 4.19 – Low vs. high depth settings for an LFO set to a square wave

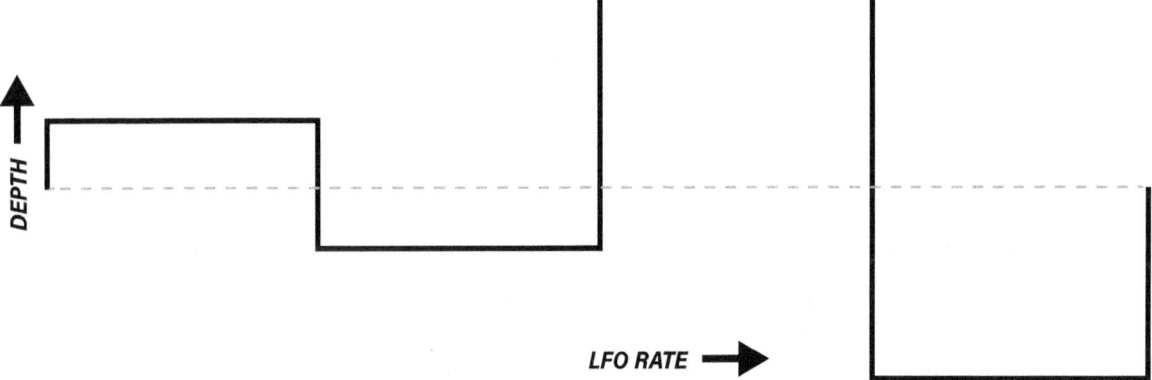

It is useful to consider that at low rates and high amounts, LFO modulation effects will follow the curves of the waveforms noticeably. For example, LFO sine (or triangle) wave modulation of oscillator pitch at about 0.5 Hz will produce the sound of an American police siren, while square wave modulation of pitch at about 1 Hz produces the sound of a British police siren.

When the LFO amount control is greater than zero, LFO modulation will be heard throughout the duration of a sound. Sometimes this is not desired, as you may want to apply modulation only when it is musically significant. A good example is when you want to apply vibrato at the end of a held note. Adding vibrato for the entire duration of a note can be monotonous, but adding vibrato to just a portion of a note can be very pleasing.

Some synths provide a modulation delay control so that LFO modulation is applied to each note only after a set amount of time has elapsed. More subtle control of modulation depth over time can be achieved using a physical performance controller, such as a modulation ("mod") wheel. The performer can play notes with one hand and use the other hand to move the mod wheel forward or back to control the modulation amount. Other types of physical controllers that can be used to control modulation amount include the foot controller (pedal), breath controller, and keyboard aftertouch.

Let's look at the LFO section in Subtractor. Subtractor actually provides two LFOs, each with separate controls. Figure 4.20 shows LFO 1. Note the typical rate (frequency) and amount (depth) controls, and waveform and destination selector buttons. Also note the switch labeled Sync, a function that will synchronize the LFO rate to the tempo setting in Reason or another DAW.

Figure 4.20 – LFO 1 in Subtractor

Figure 4.21 – LFO 2 in Subtractor

Figure 4.21 shows LFO 2. Subtractor's second LFO offers a triangle wave only, but is a *polyphonic* LFO, meaning that an independent LFO cycle is generated for each note that is played, which can yield complex and subtle effects. LFO 2 also provides modulation delay, as discussed earlier, and keyboard tracking, which increases the LFO frequency progressively the higher on the keyboard you play.

Sample-and-Hold

Related to the LFO, the sample-and-hold (S/H) module has its origins with the early analog synthesizers. An analog S/H module has an input for sampling (measuring) an incoming voltage, which could be from a source or a controller, and an output for sending a control signal derived from the sampled input. The input voltage is sampled (measured) at a rate determined by a "clock" signal, which in practice was typically provided by a dedicated LFO. In other words, the clock determined the sampling rate of the incoming voltage. Figure 4.22 shows a block diagram.

Figure 4.22 – An S/H module

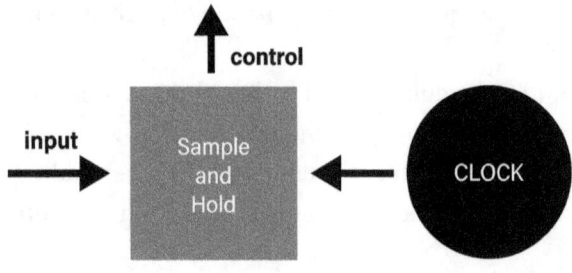

When a measurement of the incoming voltage is sampled, it is held until the next measurement is taken, hence the term "sample and hold." Since the output follows the sampled input at the rate of the clock (LFO), the output changes at regular intervals over time.

The input for the S/H module can theoretically come from most any source on a modular synthesizer, but most commonly the input source is a noise generator, which generates a random signal at the S/H output.

All this is rather technical, but in practice the S/H can be thought of simply as a source for randomized control signals that change at the rate of the associated LFO.

Figure 4.23 shows a representation of a typical control output from S/H. The circles indicate the voltage levels at which samples were taken. Notice each sample is held until the next sample is taken. The time each sample is held is determined by the clock (LFO) rate.

Figure 4.23 – The output from a S/H module that is using a noise generator

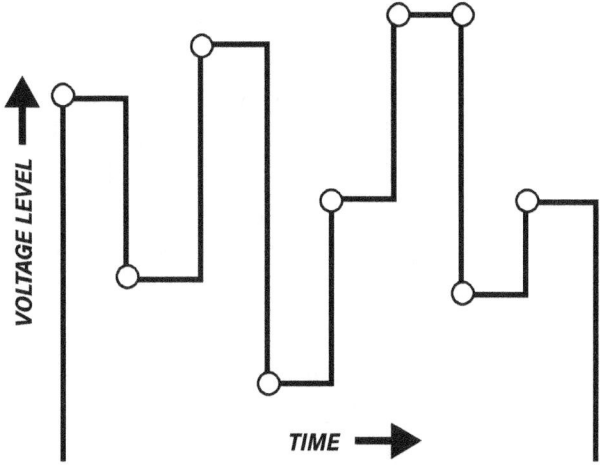

Routing the S/H output to the control input of an oscillator would cause pitch to move up a down to the shape shown in figure 4.23. Since the sampled levels are random, the pitches produced will be random as well, may even fall between notes. This effect can be difficult to use in a musical composition but will give you that random, robotic sci-fi sound so often used in old TV and films. Alternatively, routing the S/H module to the filter will cause the cutoff frequency to move up a down to the shape in figure 4.23. This effect is possibly easier to use in a musical composition, since pitch can be controlled with other means (e.g., playing the keyboard).

On most modern synthesizers, S/H simply appears as an alternate waveform for an LFO. This implementation has limitations, but greatly simplifies its application. Figure 4.24 shows LFO 1 in Subtractor. Note that the last two waveforms are sample-and-hold; the first has a normal, stepped output, while the second has a "smoothed" output where the control signal "glides" from one level to the next.

Figure 4.24 – LFO 1 in Subtractor

As mentioned, when using an oscillator for the destination of an S/H, the output will result in random pitches. If you want the effect of an S/H but with control of each pitch, use a step sequencer, a controller that allows you to set a specific pitch for each note (step).

The Keyboard

The third type of common controller is the musical keyboard. Historically, very early synthesizers did not have keyboards; however, Bob Moog added one to his voltage-controlled synthesizer in the 1960s and it has become the de facto controller for synths. Let's discuss the multiple roles for the keyboard.

Earlier in this chapter, we discussed how an EG is triggered by the keyboard. With an analog synthesizer, the attack and release stages are initiated by a gate signal. Pressing a key opens the gate signal and releasing the key closes it. For example, when a key is pressed, a +5 voltage is sent to start the EG's attack stage. The +5 voltage will be held until the key is released. This simultaneously initiates the release stage.

Figure 4.25 shows a block diagram of a keyboard connected to an amplifier EG. Some analog synthesizers also transmit a trigger signal when pressing a key. A trigger signal is a pulse that doesn't hold like a gate signal (so it doesn't trigger the release stage).

Figure 4.25 – A keyboard sending a gate signal to an amplifier EG

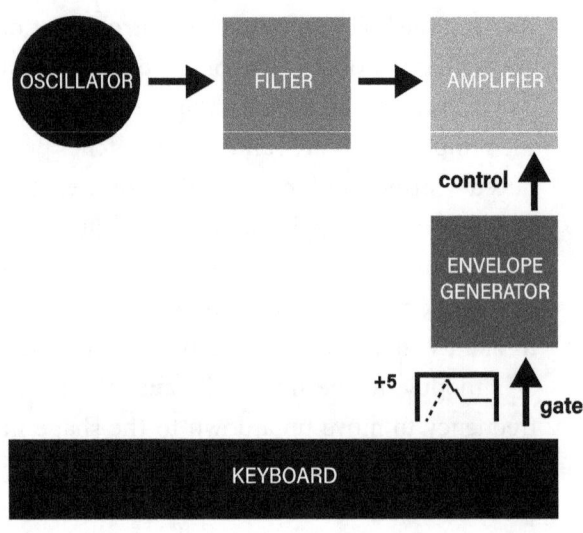

If multiple EG's are being used (e.g. a filter EG too), a gate signal will be sent to each of them. Differently, EG's on software synths (e.g. Subtractor) are triggered by MIDI messages and not a gate signal. Pressing a key on a MIDI keyboard controller transmits a MIDI Note-On message and releasing the key transmits a MIDI Note-Off message (or a MIDI Note-On message with a velocity of zero).

In addition to triggering EG's, the keyboard is responsible for changing pitch as you play different keys. In other words, as you play each key up and down the keyboard, you should hear a chromatic scale like a conventional instrument such as a piano. To accomplish this with an analog synthesizer, the keyboard sends a control voltage signal to the oscillator(s) measured at 1 volt per octave. This means that as you play each adjacent key, the voltage is changed by 1/12 of a volt (12 keys per octave). This is referred to as *Keyboard Tracking* (figure 4.26).

Figure 4.26 – A keyboard sending a control signal to the oscillator

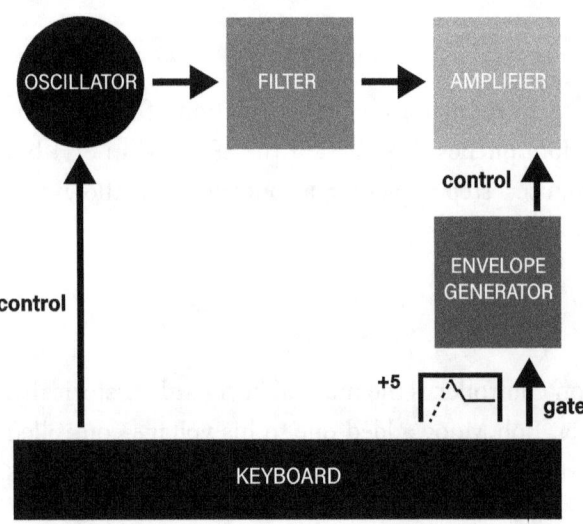

Keyboard tracking is especially useful when applied to the filter cutoff of a low pass filter. Consider that without keyboard tracking, the initial filter cutoff frequency stays the same as you move up the keyboard; therefore higher notes will sound more and more filtered and the timbre will become darker as the notes near the cutoff frequency. Sometimes this is what you want, but if not, adding keyboard tracking will increase the cutoff frequency proportionately as you play higher on the keyboard, preserving the timbre. Keyboard tracking is sometimes provided as variable control and sometimes simply a switchable function, which might have "full," "half" and "off" values. Figure 4.27 shows a block diagram.

Figure 4.27 – A keyboard sending a control signal to the filter

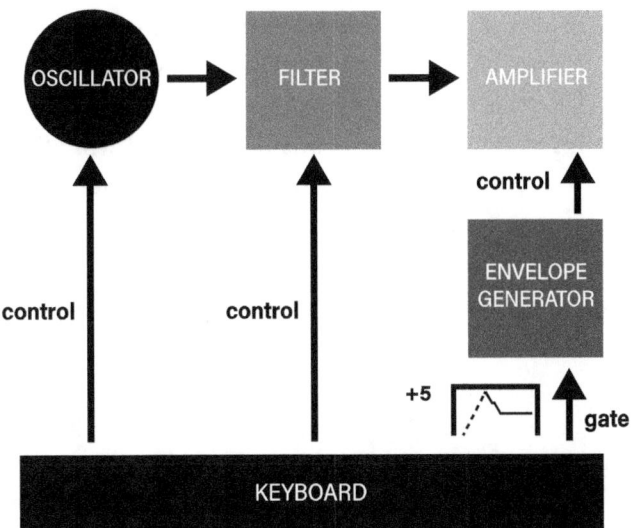

Figure 4.28 shows the keyboard tracking knob for the filters on the Voyager

Figure 4.28 – Keyboard Control Amount for the filters on the Voyager

Another very useful keyboard function is portamento or "glide." Portamento "smooths" the transition from one note to another as you play, causing the pitches to glide up and down, rather than move in discrete steps. This is a lot like a trombonist using the slide to move between notes, or a violinist slider a finger along a string. Most every synth keyboard has a portamento control, usually a simple knob or slider that allows you to adjust the speed of the portamento effect, i.e., how long it takes one note to slide to another note. Figure 4.29 shows the portamento control in Subtractor.

Figure 4.29 - The portamento control for Subtractor

Early synth keyboards were not touch sensitive in any way; they simply turned notes on and off like the keyboard of a traditional organ. In the '80s, when digital synthesizers and MIDI became common, keyboards appeared that were both velocity sensitive, like a piano, and pressure sensitive, a function called "aftertouch." Aftertouch allows the performer to press harder on the key at the bottom of its travel and control modulation effects.

A velocity sensitive keyboard measures the speed at which you strike the keys and translates this measurement into "soft" or "loud." Most modern synths will let you control the destination for the velocity control signal (most commonly the amplifier), and some will also let you adjust the velocity amount, velocity "curve" (how "soft" or "hard" the effect is), and other parameters.

Figure 4.30 show the velocity controls in Subtractor, which are very versatile. Velocity can be routed to nine possible destinations, all of which are continuously variable and can be inverted.

The Fundamentals of Synthesizer Programming

Figure 4.30 – The velocity controls in Subtractor

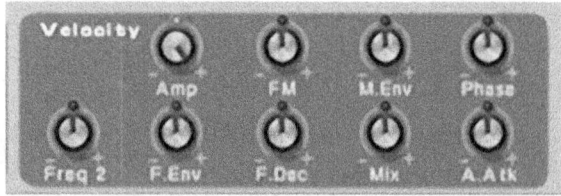

A keyboard with aftertouch measures the pressure exerted at the bottom of the key travel and translates this measurement into a control signal. Pressing down on a key as it is being played will allow you to affect patch parameters such as filter cutoff frequency or LFO amount.

Figure 4.31 shows the aftertouch controls in Subtractor. In this example, aftertouch is routed to LFO1 amount.

Figure 4.31 – The aftertouch Controls in Subtractor

Summary

In this chapter, we discussed the most common controllers, the EG, LFO, and Keyboard, and their various functions. Test your understanding by answering the questions on the next page.

Questions for Chapter 4

1. The _____ _____ is used to produce envelopes as control signals on a synthesizer.

2. To shape loudness, an envelope generator sends a control signal to a(n) _____.

3. The _____ stage determines the amount of time it takes for loudness to go from silence to maximum level.

4. The _____ stage determines how quickly the sound begins to die away after the attack stage is completed.

5. The _____ stage sets the *level* held from the end of the decay stage to key off.

6. If sustain is set to 100%, the setting for the _____ stage is irrelevant.

7. The _____ stage determines the amount of time it takes for the sound to die away after a key is released.

8. Which stage is a level setting? _____

9. The filter EG does not affect loudness, but instead controls the filter's _____ _____.

10. The filter EG's _____ control can be thought of as a kind of "range" control for the filter EG, which adjusts how much affect the envelope has on the cutoff frequency.

11. When using a filter EG, you typically want to set the cutoff frequency to a _____ frequency so you can hear it sweep the audio spectrum as it follows the envelope.

12. Is this statement True or False? Changes to your filter EG may have no effect if the amplifier EG is not set to complementary values.

13. Route an EG to a(n) _____ in order for pitch to follow an envelope as you hold a key.

14. In _____-_____ mode, the envelope generators will be triggered when a key is pressed, but will not be retriggered when other keys are pressed, until the first key is released.

15. In _____-_____ mode, the envelope generators will retrigger the attack stage with every keystroke, whether previous keys have been released or not.

16. When a(n) _____ is used as a controller, pitch, timbre or loudness will change in a cyclical, repetitive manner and follow the shape of a waveform.

17. An LFO routed to a(n) _____ will result in a change in timbre.

18. The frequency range of an LFO is typically less than 1 Hz to about _____ Hz.

19. The LFO _____ control determines the amount of change (high and low) to the destination.

20. More subtle control of LFO depth over time can be achieved using a physical performance controller, such as a _____ wheel.

21. An analog _____ module has an input for sampling (measuring) an incoming voltage, which could be from a source or a controller, and an output for sending a control signal derived from the sampled input.

22. With an analog synth, the keyboard sends a _____ signal to an EG in order to initiate its attack and release stages.

23. In order to control pitch, the keyboard sends a control voltage signal to the _____ measured at 1 volt per octave.

24. In order to control timbre, the keyboard sends a control voltage signal to the _____ _____.

25. _____ "smooths" the transition from one note to another as you play, causing the pitches to glide up and down, rather than move in discrete steps.

26. A _____ _____ keyboard measures the speed at which you strike the keys and translates this measurement into "soft" or "loud."

27. A keyboard with _____ measures the pressure exerted at the bottom of the key travel and translates this measurement into a control signal.

APPENDIX

An Overview of Electronic Music History

The evolution of technology in the twentieth century had a huge impact on music. Holmes (2002) declared that music, as we know it today, would not exist without technology. In fact, a new music, called electronic music, evolved in the twentieth century parallel to this technological evolution. This brief overview of electronic music history is divided into three sections: the beginnings, the experimental period, and the modern era.

The Beginnings

The early period occurred from around 1900 through the early 1940s, and focuses on performing electronic musical instruments. There were disagreements over when electronic music actually began. Holmes (2002) gave credit to the first electronic musical instrument to American Elisha Gray who invented the musical telegraph in 1874. Newquist (1989) and Shapiro (2000) acknowledged Thomas Edison's recording of "Mary Had A Little Lamb" on the first phonograph player in 1877 as the dawn of electronic music. However, the majority agree that electronic music began at the turn of the twentieth century with the invention of the Telharmonium by Thaddeus Cahill.

Thaddeus Cahill and the Telharmonium

Thaddeus Cahill was granted a patent in 1897 to build an electronic musical instrument and broadcast performances with telephone lines to restaurants, hotels, and private homes. His patent, "The Art of and Apparatus for Generating and Distributing Music Electronically" included the words "synthesizing" and "electrical music", foreshadowing the terms synthesizer and electronic music.

Immediately, Cahill began building an electronic instrument soon to be called the Telharmonium, and in 1901, he formed the New England Electric Music Company in Holyoke, Massachusetts. According to Chadabe (2000a) "In 1905, the New England Electric Music Company signed an agreement with the New York Telephone Company to lay special cables for the transmission of Telharmonium music throughout New York City."

In 1906, Cahill packed his 200-ton Telharmonium in twelve railway boxcars and moved it to New York City. The first public performance was at the Telharmonic Hall, and the first broadcast was later that year to a restaurant thirteen blocks away. However, telephone conversations were interrupted by the music from the Telharmonium and therefore, the telephone company terminated its agreement. As a result, the Telharmonic Hall was closed and Cahill was forced to move the Telharmonium back to Holyoke.

The Fundamentals of Synthesizer Programming

Forming the New York Cahill Telharmonic Company, Cahill made a second attempt when a franchise to lay cables for the Telharmonium by New York City was passed in 1911. However, the Telharmonium was no longer newsworthy and in 1914, Cahill declared bankruptcy.

After the Telharmonium, many other electronic instruments were built. These instruments benefited from the unique technology that vacuum tubes provided. Dobson (1998) declared the most important instruments were the theremin, the Trautonium, the Ondes Martenot, and the Hammond organ. The theremin and the Hammond organ will be further discussed.

Leon Theremin and the Theremin

According to Robert Moog (1999), "the theremin was one of the first electronic musical instruments". Leon Theremin, an engineering student in Moscow, invented the theremin in 1920. It was sometimes referred to as the aetherophone.

An unusual looking instrument, the theremin was a box with two projecting antennas; one antenna extended from the top, while the other, in a loop shape, projected horizontally from the side. Waving one hand close to the vertical antenna controlled pitch, while moving the other hand in close proximity to the horizontal antenna controlled volume. Holmes (2002) stated that the theremin operated on a modulation principle called beat frequency oscillation.

According to Chadabe (2000a), "When he arrived in New York in December of 1927, Theremin was welcomed as a celebrity". Chadabe continued, "Theremin stayed in New York for ten eventful years before returning to Russia."

The theremin was featured on the Beach Boys hit, "Good Vibrations" and on Led Zepplin's "Whole Lotta Love". In addition, it was featured in several movie soundtracks from 1940 to 1960, and in sci-fi television series, such as "Lost in Space" and the "Twilight Zone".

Laurens Hammond and the Hammond Organ

Laurens Hammond invented the Hammond organ in 1935. An ex-watchmaker and businessman, Hammond invented an electronic instrument to be mass produced and profitable. Being the first electronic instrument to be mass-produced, the Hammond organ was a commercial success with more than 5,000 sold before 1940.

The Hammond organ used the same principles as the Telharmonium; additive-synthesis through means of metal tone wheels. Crab (2005) stated that the Hammond organ had a unique drawbar system of additive timbre synthesis.

The Hammond organ has been used in everything from church choirs to daytime game shows and Chadabe (2000a) stated that the Hammond B-3 has achieved legendary status in the music world.

The Experimental Period

The experimental period was from the late 1940s to the early 1960s. There is evidence of parallel developments in electronic music. This period is broken down into three significant developments: the birth of the electronic music studio in Europe, the birth of the electronic music studio in America, and the birth of computer music.

The Birth of the Electronic Music Studio in Europe

A technological advancement that had a significant impact on electronic music was the mass marketing of the magnetic tape recorder in 1948. Until this time, electronic music had mostly been a live performance medium, but now it had also become a composer's medium. Imaginative composers began creating Tape Music, which referred to sounds that had been recorded on tape, then rearranged and organized into a complete composition. This initiated many tape techniques such as tape splicing, tape echo, tape delay, and tape looping.

Two European broadcasting networks, Radiodiffusion Television Francis (RTF) in Paris and Norwetdeutscher Rundfunk (NWDR) in Cologne, Germany, formed electronic music studios that used the tape recorder, but with different approaches. RTF called their approach musique concrete while NWDR called their approach electronic music.

In 1948, while working as an electro-acoustic engineer at the RTF, Pierre Schaeffer recorded various sounds from trains and organized them into a short composition he named *Railroad Study*. To describe his technique, he coined the term musique concrete. Musique concrete was defined by Rhea (1988a) as "the manipulation and mixing of natural or 'concrete' sounds recorded with a microphone".

It should be noted that Pierre Schaffer used plastic discs, rather than magnetic tape, for *Railroad Study*. It wasn't until 1951 when Pierre Schaffer and many others at RTF began to use the magnetic tape recorder and the aforementioned tape techniques.

The other aforementioned European electronic music studio that emerged at this time was the NWDR in Cologne, Germany. Differently than the composers at RTF, the composers at NWDR referred to their approach as electronic music meaning that pieces were produced from electronic sources rather than natural sources. Also differently from RTF, one particular person did not pioneer electronic music at NWDR. However, literature predominately mentions Karlheinz Stockhausen who came to NWDR in 1953 and became the studio's director and principle composer.

The composers at NWDR initially used an additive synthesis approach with a single sine wave oscillator and a four-track tape recorder. This laborious process was soon enhanced with electronic instruments such as the Monochord and the Melochord.

The Birth of the Electronic Music Studio in America

On October 28, 1952, composers Otto Luening and Vladimir Ussachevsky presented the first public concert of Tape Music in the United States at the Museum of Modern Art in New York. Following their success, they made a formal proposal to Columbia University to establish an electronic music studio, which materialized in 1955.

In 1956, RCA unveiled the new Mark I Electronic Music Synthesizer in New York. Constructed by Harry Olsen and Herbert Belar, it was 20 feet in length, reached from floor to ceiling, and data was entered via punched paper roll. Luening, Ussachevsky, and Princeton University professor Milton Babbit, became interested in the RCA synthesizer and applied to the Rockefeller Foundation for a grant that to finance a new studio to house the synthesizer. In 1959, a grant for $175,000 was awarded for a joint studio between Columbia and Princeton. It became known as the Columbia-Princeton Electronic Music Center at Columbia University, and housed the improved RCA Mark II Electronic Music Synthesizer. Over the next ten years, over sixty composers came to work there. Luening (1968) stated the following: "The Columbia-Princeton Electronic Music Center was the first American electronic collaborative academic effort focusing on electronic music. We wanted to provide a center where composers could work and experiment without having to contend with the forces of commercialism. At the same time you could feed it to students and make the studio available for people to work in, to experiment on a high level."

Chadabe (1997) stated that the idea of Tape Music was so powerful that electronic music studios spread throughout the world. However, "because equipment was expensive and technical knowledge was necessary, most of the first studios were established at institutions where budgets and technicians were available". By 1966, there were 560 known institutional and private studios in the world and an institution of some type sponsored approximately 40% of them.

The Birth of Computer Music

The first commercial computers were the UNIVAC in 1951 and IBM 701 in 1953. These large computers were mainframe machines. In 1957, Max Mathews, an engineer at Bell Telephone Laboratories in Murry Hill, New Jersey, demonstrated the first computer-generated sound. This was accomplished with his computer synthesis program, MUSIC I. Over the next several years, Max Mathews and his collaborators at Bell Labs released improved versions of Music I that were referred to as the Music N series. For example, a later version, Music V, was introduced in 1968.

Many significant developments grew from the research at Bell Labs. John Chowning, a graduate student at Stanford University, visited Bell Labs in 1963. Chowning returned to Stanford with MUSIC IV to establish a laboratory for computer music with David Poole. Chowning made a major breakthrough in 1971 when be developed a digital synthesis technique called FM (frequency modulation). FM was licensed by Yamaha in 1974 and was successfully used for commercial digital synthesizers in the 1980s.

By the end of the 1970s, MUSIC V programs were installed in many American universities. However, musicians had to know computer programming to compose computer music with these programs.

The Modern Era

The modern era covers from the early 1960s to about year 2000. It is divided into six sections: the birth of the synthesizer, the development of the synthesizer in 1970s, the development of digital instruments, the birth of the Musical Instrument Digital Interface (MIDI), the development of personal computer hardware and software, and electronic dance music.

The Birth of the Synthesizer

Although the RCA Mark II Electronic Music Synthesizer was introduced in 1956, a majority described the first synthesizer appearing in the early 1960s parallel to the introduction of transistors and voltage-control.

Eisengrein (2004) defined the synthesizer as a transducer that translates electrical energy into sound. Differently, Holmes (2002) defined the synthesizer as a device that was designed to generate purely electronic sounds by analog or digital means. Rhea (1972) stated that most synthesizers are designed for subtractive synthesis; a type of synthesis that modifies complex waves with various types of filters.

The first synthesizers were analog modular systems that used voltage control. Three different men invented the synthesizer independently: Robert Moog in New York, Donald Buchla in San Francisco, and Paul Ketoff in Rome. However, a majority gave credit to Robert Moog. His invention was considered the most traditional because it had a keyboard resembling a traditional piano.

Moog began his construction of a synthesizer for the composer Herbert Deutsch. This synthesizer became a collection of separate modules (e.g. an oscillator, filter, amplifier, envelope generator) that was connected with patch cords. In Robert Moog's (1999) own words: "The modular electronic music synthesizers of the 1960s made by companies such as Buchla, Moog, and others combined some of the tone production and control features of theremins and other early instruments with the sorts of sound generation and processing that were developed by the post-World War II tape composers. Using the technical principle of voltage-control, these large, telephone-switchboard-like instruments enabled musicians to shape and sequence sounds automatically and by purely electronic means."

The sound of Moog's large modular synthesizers of the 1960s, was popularized by the 1968 release of Wendy Carlos' *Switched on Bach*; an all-synthesizer album that became the top-selling classical music of all time. In addition, Keith Emerson of the rock band Emerson, Lake and Palmer used a Moog modular synthesizer to perform a lead solo on the 1969 hit recording of "Lucky Man."

Around 1970, there was an emerging commercial interest in electronic music. Previously, nearly all of Moog's customers were composers from universities. However, the musicians recording and performing with these instruments gradually shifted from academia to more mainstream musical genres. Because of this, the focus for synthesizer design moved from academic composer needs to commercial artist needs.

The Development of the Synthesizer in the 1970s

Advancements in technology during the post-war period had a tremendous impact on electronic music. The vacuum tube of the 1950s gave way to the transistor in the 1960s. The integrated circuit and microprocessor appeared in the 1970s. These technological achievements resulted in a decrease in size, cost and complexity for computers and synthesizers.

Demand from musicians led to a large number of companies with new simplified, portable synthesizers. In 1969, ARP Instruments was formed and released the modular Model 2500. Marketed to schools, it was a fraction of the size and cost of the large modular synthesizers that preceded it. But the first commercially portable synthesizer was Moog's MiniMoog introduced in 1970. Unlike the modular synthesizers that came before, it did not require patch cables. Rhea explains (1988b), "all the control voltage routings were accomplished with switches and knobs".

These small, portable analog synthesizers still had two limitations. First, they were monophonic, meaning that only one note could be sounded at a time, and second, every time a different sound was desired, switches and knobs on the panel had to be painstakingly adjusted. These two problems were soon to disappear. The first polyphonic synthesizer, the Oberheim Four Voice, was introduced in 1975 allowing for multiple notes (chords) to sound simultaneously for the first time. Soon after, the first programmable monophonic synthesizer, the OB-1, was introduced in 1977 allowing different sounds, also known as patches, to be recalled from memory with the single push of a button. Finally, polyphony and programmability were combined in the first fully programmable polyphonic synthesizer in 1978 with the popular Sequential Circuits Prophet-5.

The Development of Digital Musical Instruments

By 1980, the introduction of the Synclavier and the Fairlight CMI signaled the dawn of a new era of all digital instruments. However, this impact was only felt at the high-end market. For example, a fully equipped Synclavier in the early 1980s cost more than $200,000. With state-of-the-art synthesis and sampling, they were only affordable by institutions and up-scale studios.

Following the introduction of the Synclavier and Farilight CMI, digital instruments divided into two branches: synthesizers and samplers. Down the synthesizer branch, the Yamaha DX7, in 1983, was the first commercially viable digital synthesizer. Verderosa (2002) indicated its popularity, "The DX7 became the fastest selling and most popular synthesizer in history". It was so popularity because it incorporated MIDI (Musical Instrument Digital Interface), sounded good, had 16-note polyphony, and was priced for less than $2,000. Gerrish (2001) stated that the DX7 was a pivotal shift from analog to all-digital synthesizers. In addition, "The digital keyboard became an essential piece of gear for anyone interested in electronic music". The DX7 used the aforementioned FM synthesis technique that John Chowning invented at Stanford University in 1971. FM and other techniques were used for digital synthesizers throughout the 1980s and 1990s. However, many people turned to samplers due to their ability to digitally record and playback any sound.

During this time, technology was advancing quickly and prices were dropping rapidly. In a five-year period, the price of a digital sampler dropped from $25,000 for a Fairlight CMI in 1979, to $10,000 for an E-mu Emulator in 1981, to less than $1,300 for an Ensoniq Mirage in 1984. By 1988, Ensoniq had sold 30,000 Mirage samplers. According to Kettlewel (2002), digital samplers had become one of the most significant tools for electronic music. They were able to replay a digitally stored sample (recording) whenever triggered by a note. In addition, samples could be edited with various techniques such as looping, pitch shifting, and crossfading. These editing techniques are analogous to the aforementioned tape editing techniques that were used for musique concrete. Verderosa (2002) said that samplers allowed composers to playback more accurate representations of acoustic instruments.

The Birth of MIDI

By the late 1970s, the number of manufacturers for electronic music instruments had grown to include American companies such as Moog, Arp, E-mu, Sequential Circuits, Oberheim, and many Japanese companies such as Roland, Korg, Yamaha and Kawai. However, on a control level, a product from one company could not communicate with another. Therefore, you had to buy products from the same company to ensure compatibility for communication.

During June of 1981, the idea of a standard for digital communication between electronic music devices was discussed between Ikutaro Kakehashi of Roland, Tom Oberheim of Oberheim, and Dave Smith of Sequential Circuits. In October, a meeting was arranged with representatives from Korg, Yamaha and Kawai. Following, in November, Dave Smith proposed the Universal Synthesizer Interface (USI) at the Audio Engineering Society (AES) convention in New York. The name was changed to Musical Instrument Digital Interface (MIDI) while being further refined throughout 1982. In January 1983, MIDI was first demonstrated at the National Association for Musical Merchants (NAMM) show when a Roland JP-6 synthesizer successfully communicated with a Sequential Circuits Prophet 600 synthesizer. Audio could be heard coming from both synthesizer keyboards whenever a person played just one of them. In August of 1983, the MIDI 1.0 specification was published.

The Personal Computer and Development of Software

Webster (2002) stated that during this period, "we witnessed the growth of small, but powerful, personal computer systems". Holmes (2002) added, "the personal computer has become an essential component of the electronic musician's equipment arsenal". The first personal computers, such as the Apple II and the Commodore 64, appeared in the late 1970s and were adequate for some music applications. The IBM

PC, which was introduced in 1981, was regarded by many sectors of the computing industry as little more than a tool for hobbyists. A turning point for music occurred with the introduction of the Macintosh.

In January of 1984 Apple Computer introduced the Macintosh computer. Its easy to use graphical interface was well suited for musical applications and therefore became the choice platform for musicians. Incorporating MIDI, music applications were being written for the Commodore 64, the Atari ST-series and the IBM PC, but the Macintosh became the leading platform.

The year 1985 saw a rapid growth in MIDI software developers. Introducing many different types of applications, the most common application was the MIDI sequencer. Modeled after a multi-track tape recorder, it allowed the recording and playback of MIDI information with MIDI devices such as an electronic keyboard. Leading companies for the MIDI sequencer were established at this time; Opcode Systems, Mark of the Unicorn and Steinberg. Other types of MIDI software introduced at this time included patch editors, music notation, auto-composers, automatic accompaniment, music theory and ear-training programs.

Having nothing to do with MIDI, the first digital audio programs appeared in 1985 as editor programs for samplers. The first serious digital audio program to be an alternative to a two-track tape recorder was Digidesign's SoundTools introduced in 1988. Then in 1990, a milestone development occurred when Opcode combined MIDI sequencing and digital audio in the same environment. This started a new family of software that is still common today with programs such as Digital Performer, Pro Tools, Cubase SX and Logic Pro.

The launch of Microsoft Windows 95 provided a Graphic User Interface (GUI) for the PC platform that met the essential requirements for modern personal computing. By the year 2000, Windows had a repertory of music software finally to rival that available for the Apple Macintosh. Both the Macintosh and IBM-type machines had become the dominant computers for music performance and education.

In 1996, Steinberg developed VST (Virtual Studio Technology) for the ability to add audio effects and processing as plug-ins to their digital audio sequencer, Cubase VST. This technology became a standard and in 1999, the release of VST 2.0 pioneered the development for software synthesizers and samplers. Russ (2004) stated that by the beginning of the 21st century, software was able to emulate synthesizers and samplers, and the comparatively low cost of software to hardware allowed many more people to explore sound design with synthesizers and samplers.

By 2000, it is clear that a world previously dominated by hardware products is fast becoming more supportive for computer-based systems offering facilities based on software rather than hardware.

Electronic Dance Music

This genre of music has spawned many new electronic music techniques such as turntabelism and remixing. According to Verderosa (2002), the DJ was the driving force for this movement. It has birthed a plethora of electronic music sub-genres such as techno, house, electro, jungle, and breakbeat.

References and Further Reading for History

Barroso, K., & Niles, N. (2003). Electronic music time line. Retrieved May 31, 2005, from http://www.intuitivemusic.com/techno-guide-time-line.html

Chadabe, J. (1997). Electric sound. Upper Saddle River, NJ: Prentice Hall.

Chadabe, J. (2000a). The electronic century part 1: Beginnings. Electronic Musician Retrieved May 31, 2005, from http://emusician.com/mag/emusic_electronic_century_part_3/index.html

Chadabe, J. (2000c). The electronic century part 3: Computers and analog synthesizers. Electronic Musician Retrieved June 4, 2005, from http://emusician.com/mag/emusic_electronic_century_part_2/index.html

Crab, S. (2005). 120 years of electronic music. Retrieved June 2, 2005, from http://www.obsolete.com/120_years/

Dobson, R. (1998). A dictionary of electronic and computer music technology. New York: Oxford University Press.

Eisengrein, D. (2004, September 1). From vcos to dcos. Remix Retrieved May 27, 2005, from http://remixmag.com/mag/remix_vcos_dcos/index.html

Gerrish, B. (2001). Remix: The electronic music explosion. Vallejo, CA: EM Books.

Holmes, T. (2002). Electronic and experimental music (2nd ed.). New York, NY: Routledge.

Kettlewell, B. (2002). Electronic music pioneers. Vallejo, CA: ProMusic Press.

Luening, O. (1968). An unfinished history of electronic music. In T. Ziegler & J. Gross (Eds.), Ohm: The early gurus of electronic music (pp. 43). Roslyn, NY: Ellipsis Arts.

Manning, P. (2004). Electronic and computer music (Revised and expanded ed.). New York: Oxford University Press.

Moog, R. (1999). The theremin and the synthesizer. In T. Ziegler & J. Gross (Eds.), Ohm: The early gurus of electronic music (pp. 19). Roslyn, NY: Ellipsis Arts.

Newquist, H. P. (1989). Music and technology. New York: Billboard Books.

Rhea, T. (1972). The evolution of electronic musical instruments in the united states. Unpublished Dissertation, George Peabody College for Teachers.

Rhea, T. (1988a). What is electronic music? In B. Hurtig (Ed.), Synthesizer basics (pp. 1¬2). Milwaukee: Hal Leonard Books.

Rhea, T. (1988b). Moog, buchla & beyond. In B. Hurtig (Ed.), Synthesizer basics. Milwaukee: Hal Leonard Books.

Russ, M. (2004). Sound, synthesis and sampling. Burlington, MA: Focal Press.

Shapiro, P. (2000). Modulations. New York: Caipirinha Productions.

Verderosa, T. (2002). The techno primer. Milwaukee: Hal Leonard Books.

Webster, P. R. (2002). Historical perspectives on technology and music. Music Educators Journal, 89, 38-43.

Questions for Electronic Music History

1. _____ _____ was granted a patent in 1897 to build an electronic musical instrument that became known as the Telharmonium.

2. _____ _____ an engineering student in Moscow, invented the theremin in 1920.

3. _____ _____ invented the Hammond organ in 1935.

4. Pierre Schaeffer recorded various sounds from trains and organized them into a short composition he named Railroad Study. To describe his technique, he coined the term _____ _____.

5. In 1959, the Columbia-Princeton Electronic Music Center at Columbia University housed the _____.

6. _____ _____ made a major breakthrough in 1971 when be developed a digital synthesis technique called FM (frequency modulation) that was licensed by Yamaha in 1974.

7. Primary credit is given to _____ _____ as the inventor of the first voltage controlled synthesizers.

8. The sound of Moog's large modular synthesizers of the 1960s, was popularized by the 1968 release of Wendy Carlos' _____ _____ _____, and by a lead solo on the 1969 hit recording of _____ _____.

9. The first commercially portable synthesizer was Moog's _____ introduced in 1970.

10. The first fully _____ _____ synthesizer was introduced in 1978 as the popular Sequential Circuits Prophet-5.

11. The Yamaha DX7, in 1983, was the first commercially viable _____ synthesizer.

12. In August of 1983 the _____ 1.0 specification was published.

13. In January of 1984 Apple Computer introduced the _____ computer.

14. In 1990, a milestone development occurred when Opcode combined MIDI sequencing and _____ _____ in the same environment (software).

Notes